GRIFFITH AND THE RISE OF HOLLYWOOD
by Paul O'Dell

Above: Robert Harron

In the same series, produced by THE TANTIVY PRESS and edited by Peter Cowie:

GRIFFITH AND THE RISE OF HOLLYWOOD

by PAUL O'DELL
(with the assistance of Anthony Slide)

THE INTERNATIONAL FILM GUIDE SERIES
A. S. BARNES & CO., NEW YORK
A. ZWEMMER LIMITED, LONDON

Acknowledgements

I WISH TO THANK the following for the help and assistance that they have given to me in the preparation of this book: Kevin Brownlow, Leslie Flint, John Lanchbery, Bert Langdon, Jill O'Dell, Anthony Slide and, above all, Harold Dunham.

The chapter on Thomas H. Ince was prepared with the special help of Mrs. Thomas Ince and George C. Pratt of George Eastman House.

COVER STILLS
Front: David Wark Griffith
Back: Mary Pickford

FIRST PUBLISHED 1970
Copyright © 1970 by Paul O'Dell
Library of Congress Catalog Card No. 71-119640
SBN 302-02060-8 (U.K.)
SBN 498-07718-7 (U.S.A.)

Printed in the United States of America

Contents

1. Introduction

DAVID WARK GRIFFITH HAS TENDED TO BECOME, in recent years, a figure in cinema history attributed with innovation in film technique; the close-up, the flashback, cross-cutting have all appeared in connection with his name. And so it is that he is now in danger of achieving a widespread reputation merely as a technician: an inventor of cinematography. This does justice neither to Griffith himself nor to his work. It may very well be that he did "invent" all these ideas of pictorial presentation—but there is much evidence to suggest that he did not—and if he did not, then he certainly developed their use to startling effect. But these ideas, these techniques were for him only a means towards an end; never the ultimate distinguishing factor of his pictures. Nor was he dependent on these techniques in order to produce a film which stood above all contemporary works. Many of his early pictures contain no close-ups, no flashbacks, no camera movement, no complicated editing techniques, and no innovations. But nevertheless they are indisputably films of high artistic quality. Many post-*Intolerance* films also contain few, if any, of the "innovations" attributed to Griffith, and yet they are outstanding works nonetheless.

It is unfortunate—indeed it could be tragic—that a man who strove so hard to perfect the cinema as a medium for the stimulation of *ideas* should also have been the one who recognised the real potential of an embryo art form. The fact remains that while the technical achievements of D. W. Griffith have become the main reason for his importance in film history, his purely artistic achievements, the very reason why he ever made films at all, have tended to become relatively obscured.

The work of an artist is the door to his soul: whatever we see written about the artist, we will never get closer to the man himself than through his work. David Wark Griffith produced a tremendous volume of work during the twenty-three years he spent making motion pictures. It is via these films—those that remain—that we can come to a real understanding of Griffith, because into these films he poured all of his ideas

Griffith (right) and Bitzer filming the climax of the Modern Story in Intolerance. *In the car Mae Marsh and Miriam Cooper with Tod Browning at the wheel.*

and life. In many cases he drew from personal experience for his insight into certain situations or characters, and projected himself into his work through actors and actresses who could not help but respond to his forceful yet genuine character. In his pictures we can understand this character—the unmistakable *Griffith style.*

Griffith was a man of ambition, and he achieved much during his active life in the film industry. In all his published articles, he talked continually, not of ways and means, not how a film is made, not of film *form,* but of *ideas,* and the importance of conveying ideas through the exciting new medium of film.

The respect he gained from those who worked with him gives us further indication that his best work is a great deal more than simply commercial venture (although it was often this as well) or technical expertise—which it certainly never was. It is first and foremost a testimony—and this could never have been had not his artistes become infused with, and eager to share his incredible enthusiasm for picture-making. Mae Marsh, for example, who gave in *Intolerance* one of her most memorable performances, had for Griffith "the strong and mixed feeling that the child has for its benefactor, or the student for a beloved preceptor."[1] She echoes others who worked with him when she says "no matter how well we think we have outlined a scene Mr. Griffith may entirely change it. When he does change it we know it is for a reason other than a fondness for showing authority. In other words, he has built up among his artists a great and abiding faith in his ability to do the right thing at the right time, or, as importantly, have it done."[1]

Griffith rode at the head of the motion picture industry's development from cheap amusement to sophisticated and accepted means of communication. It was he, after all, who did so much to promote the medium. But, eventually and inevitably, he found himself attacked from all sides and very soon expelled from Hollywood once his particular genius became swamped by the new generation of movie-makers and the big business which came with them. Perhaps it is to his credit that he did not try to mould himself to their ideas of how pictures should be made. Even today, the reaction against Griffith remains. He is criticised in retrospect for his "extrovert sentimentality," and it is still claimed, as it was forty years ago, that his pictures sink into absurdity simply because he never held any regard for the rule that true life transposed directly to the screen often appears false. I do not intend to suggest that Griffith was entirely innocent of such criticisms, but I do firmly believe that he did *what* he did genuinely, and straight from the heart. For this reason alone his work is worthy of more attention and serious study than has been afforded it in the past. His best films are passionate and tender, terrifying and poignant, works of art certainly, and products too of an imagination far ahead of its time in the medium of motion pictures.

The great irony of Griffith's contribution to the development of the cinema as a legitimate art form was that he had no ambition in the direction of moving pictures when, as a young man, he arrived in New York in the early 1900s. by this time, Edwin Stratton Porter had already made *The Great Train Robbery* and *The Life of an American Fireman,* both important films in the development of the cinema, and public interest in the moving picture was beginning to gain momentum. There still remained, however, a certain quality of disregard associated with films, especially among the acting profession—of which Griffith was at that time a member—who, naturally enough, saw them as a perversion of theatrical performance. In actual fact, they were little more than just that, although films such as those mentioned above were trying to break loose from the theatrical tradition that still tended to filter through into film studios. Filmed plays were still popular. The cinema had already developed its basic techniques for story-telling. The close-up had been used extensively, if not successfully, and many other devices for heightening dramatic effect had already been experimented with. What the moving picture business badly wanted was the man who was able to weld all these factors coherently and by so doing lift the medium from the restrictions of theatrical presentation.

D. W. Griffith, or "Lawrence" Griffith as he then called himself (he was reserving his proper name for greater things) found himself with no alternative but to approach a film company for work. As an actor, he was having little success in New York. The Edison company hired him and he appeared as the leading male role in a film called *Rescued from an Eagle's Nest,* a second-best alternative when Edwin S. Porter, then head of Edison, refused to buy a script from him.

Griffith's ambition had always been to become a distinguished author. It was for this that he reserved his right name of David Wark. He had worked on a local newspaper in his native Southland, toured with a theatrical company to New York, and had written several plays, poems and stories. He had, by the time he approached Edison, already had one play produced—only to close a failure within two weeks—and a poem published. The great Southern pride of David Wark Griffith must have been shattered indeed when he was forced to act in movies, then the lowest profession to which any actor could sink.

But when, a little later, he approached the Biograph company, his literary efforts met with a qualified success and he became permanently employed there, primarily as an actor but occasionally as a writer of scripts. Griffith's employ at the American Mutoscope and Biograph Company, documented in *Early American Cinema* (the first volume in this series), ended with Griffith making bigger and more ambitious pictures until the business nerve of the Biograph's management began to crack. They suppressed his later films; *The Massacre* (1912) had been held back from distribution in America simply, it would appear, because it was in two reels instead of the nominal one. *The Battle at Elderbush Gulch* and *Brute Force* (both 1913) had been shelved for the same reason. And *Judith of Bethulia* (1913) in four reels was so outrageously gargantuan as to be considered positively indigestible by the public.

Being a pioneer in the true sense of the word, Griffith found that his employers were extremely wary of his bold approach to picture production. They became critical of his budget for films and saw nothing but lack of print sales at the end of the path their *enfant terrible* was treading. It was only after the success of *The Birth of a Nation* that they re-issued his films, now carrying his name—which they never did previously.

After his departure from Biograph, Griffith supervised the releases from the Reliance-Majestic studios, and during 1914 he directed four features for that company: *The Battle of the Sexes, Home Sweet Home, The Escape* and *The Avenging Conscience*. But, during the summer of that year he at last began work on the project he had been considering for some time previously, an adaptation of the Rev. Thomas Dixon's novel, *The Clansman*.

The picture was first seen by the public on the evening of February 8, 1915. It opened early in the next month in New York, this time with the title it was to bear for good, *The Birth of a Nation*.

After a gap of fifty-five years, the picture is still a textbook of cinematic technique and dramatic application. It was the film in which Griffith brought together all the strands of the film-maker's art which he had observed, or stumbled across, or developed, during his years with the American Biograph. The beginning of 1915, with the film's *première*, was the beginning of the cinema's adulthood.

It is impossible to consider *The Birth of a Nation* without resorting to these well-used phrases. Such is the film's importance. But apart from its place in the history books of the cinema, there is another consideration we have to make. The picture has been the centre of endless and continuous discussion, not to mention questioning and downright condemnation, as a result of the more inflammatory aspects of its subject matter. Griffith now found himself, after five years of virtual anonymity, suddenly both acclaimed as a genius and condemned as a despicable racialist. Eileen Bowser observed that *"The Birth of a Nation* is probably the only film of its period which can still move an audience to the heights of emotion. This may account for endless controversies about its message, for other films, such as Lubin's *Coon Town Suffragettes* and Turner's *In Slavery Days,* which are much more blatantly racist, have long since been forgotten. It is not easy to be objective about *The Birth of a Nation* today. It must be kept in mind that the film was a Southerner's honest effort to portray events still very close to the experience of the community in which he grew up. Griffith had the native attitudes of the Southern tradition. At the same time he was a Nineteenth century romantic. But above all he was a dramatist: he was a genius at portraying emotion by means of the language of the screen."[2] It cannot be denied, however, that the forcefulness of the film impresses upon the viewer the idea that the Negro race is an inferior one; that confronted with responsibility it is incapable of being responsible; that it is gullible and that it should be repressed. These are issues which the film raises with the infinitely more liberal viewer of the Seventies; but they are clouds which only serve to distract his attention from the broader issues with which Griffith's film is more importantly concerned. Griffith himself proved time and again his tolerance and understanding and always stressed the importance in his films of the representation of what he called "Brotherly Love."

The following brief analysis of the picture—and the more comprehensive analysis of *Intolerance* which follows it—may help to put the film in a clearer perspective; but any written description of this film or for that matter any of Griffith's other pictures, cannot help but be pale commentaries on the films themselves. Without the staggering visual momentum which makes the picture the masterpiece it undoubtedly is, this analysis hopes to convey Griffith's "honest effort to portray events."

2. The Birth of a Nation

THE FILM BEGINS with a series of titles. The penultimate of these contains sentiments which Griffith elaborated upon in an article some twelve months after the picture's completion. The title reads: "If in this work we have conveyed to the mind the ravages of war to the end that *war may be held in abhorrence,* this effort will not have been in vain." In the English trade journal *Kine Year Book* issue of 1916, there appeared an article by Griffith, in which he said, apropos of *The Birth of a Nation*:

> "When one realises to what an extent the biggest evils of our present-day civilisation—such a war as is now in progress for example—are due to a lack of imaginative vision, the enormous power the cinema-play possesses as an educator (while not losing its powers as a medium of entertainment) are obvious. *The Birth of a Nation* does not profess to be a sermon, but if, incidentally, it does something to show the real character of 'glorious war' it will, I think, have served at least one useful purpose."

Quite apart from stating his position as an advocate of peace and tolerance, this piece also demonstrates how Griffith thoroughly understood that his medium had two facets and both were powerful and capable of gross misuse. It is also interesting to note that he sees the cinema first as an educative medium, and secondly, but nonetheless importantly, as a "medium of entertainment."

Following the introductory titles, the film's main narrative is preceded with a brief historical prologue, the scene of which is set by the title, "The bringing of the African to America planted the first seeds of disunion." This contains scenes of Negroes being sold as slaves, and Abolitionists advocating the freeing of all slaves. The sixth shot of this three-hour film is of a white man and Negro child: one man protesting the inequality of his fellow man, irrespective of his colour or religion.

After this, *The Birth of a Nation* as a visual drama gets under way properly. A title sets the year as 1860 and we are introduced to the two families who are to participate in, endure and ride the private, public and national crises with which the film concerns itself. The Northern family, the Stonemans, consist of Austin Stoneman (Ralph Lewis), his daughter Elsie (Lillian Gish) and his two sons Phil (Elmer Clifton) and Tod (Bobby Harron). The Southern family, who have known the Stonemans and who are paid a visit by them in the opening passages of the film, consist of young Ben Cameron, whom we first see returning to their large house in Piedmont (played by Henry B. Walthall); on the porch of the house is his elder sister Margaret (Miriam Cooper), his father, described in a title as "The kindly master of Cameron Hall" (Spottiswoode Aiken) and his younger sister Flora (Violet Wilkes, played later by Mae Marsh).

There is a passage in the opening sequences so typical of Griffith's pictures; and sequences of a similar nature can be found in nearly all of his major films and quite a few of his lesser films also. We have already seen Lillian Gish playing with a kitten during the scenes in which Tod and Phil were composing a letter to the Camerons; and now, on the porch of the Cameron house, the two sisters and their father play with young puppies. Several close-ups are not too extravagant an indulgence in the immediate appeal of animals for Griffith—indeed it symbolised for him a certain quality of innocence and contentment which he hoped would infuse these introductory sequences with a similar atmosphere. He has, in this instance, a kitten dropped on top of the puppies, which, following the title, "Hostilities," results in the baring of teeth, and could possibly be a subtle intrusion into the calm atmosphere of these scenes of the change of mood which the film is eventually to adopt. But this is not too forcibly suggested, and the scene is passed over quickly.

Elsie is unable to join her brothers on their visit to the South; but her photograph provides Ben with the young romantic's ideal woman, and the younger brothers of each family particularly find each other's company a source of great happiness: the title, "Chums—the younger sons. North and South," underlines the senselessness of what we know is about to take place and gives the scene a touching ironic undertone.

Griffith's love of the romantic image is given full rein during these sequences, and the titles help to further the atmosphere: Phil Stoneman and Margaret Cameron for example walk "Over the plantation to the cotton fields" but do so "By Way of Love Valley."

Miriam Cooper as Margaret Cameron

14

What might be called the political element of the film now begins to take shape as the story turns to Washington and Austin Stoneman's "weakness that is to blight a nation" (title). After a brush with Charles Sumner, the leader of the Senate, Stoneman's mulatto housekeeper Lydia Brown (Mary Alden) is found in tears by him. He tries to put his arms around her but she draws away. The title, "The first call for 7,500 volunteers—President Lincoln signing the proclamation" precedes one of the many "historical facsimiles" that appear throughout the film, with references to sources also included in titles. This particular scene carries with it a great dignity especially in the closing moments when Joseph Henabery's sensitive acting gives the great statesman a touching credibility as he pulls a handkerchief out and after wiping his brow, bows his head in prayer.

After several scenes announcing the onset of war, the picture jumps forward two years, and there follow the first scenes of war itself. Ben Cameron's younger sister, now grown into a young woman (and played now by Mae Marsh) has put on her last decent dress in honour of a letter from her brother at the front. Both she and her sister are about to go for a walk when the town is raided by an "irregular guerrilla force." The sisters and the rest of the family take shelter in a basement —the father staying to fight, however—and as the soldiers run to and fro above them the Little Sister begins to smile, then laugh as her excitement and semi-comprehension of the situation rise to the surface. Mae Marsh herself explains in her autobiography how this scene, which conveys beautifully the drama and tension of the situation through what might be called *counter-dramatic* terms, was arrived at:

" . . . it was a matter of some moment how the Little Sister, which part I was fortunate enough to play, would be affected. I can hear your average director: 'Roll your eyes' he would say, 'Cry! Drop to your knees in terror!' In other words, it would be the same old stuff. . . .
Mr. Griffith, when we came to the cellar scene, asked me if there had been a time in my life when I had been filled with terror. 'Yes.' I said. 'What did you do?' he enquired.

Mae Marsh as The Little Sister

'I laughed' I answered. He saw the point immediately. 'Good' he said, 'let's try it.'
It was the hysterical laugh of the little girl in the cellar, with the drunken mob raging above, that was I am sure, far more effective than rolling the eyes or weeping would have been."[1]

A company of Confederate troops relieves the town, and the scene shifts to Ben, "The Little Colonel," reading a letter from home, which itself carries obvious dramatic weight, since he is unaware of the danger that has threatened his family. We then see the first scenes of action on the battlefield, preceded with the title, "War claims its *bitter, useless* sacrifice. True to their promise, the chums meet again." This title refers back to the scene when the two youngest sons of both families left each other's company in Piedmont, promising that they would see each other again soon. The young Cameron is shot and wounded during a charge, and Tod Stoneman rushes up to bayonet the dying soldier. He stops suddenly as he realises who it is, frozen in mid-action. As he stands there, speechless, he himself is shot and falls across his young friend's body. In such a position they die together, and this is one of Griffith's most poignant and telling attacks on the horrors and obscenities of war, but done not in an attacking manner. The scene is simple, relying on the intensity of individual performers and the knowledge that the audience has already been given concerning these two characters.

The Cameron family read of their youngest son's death on "War's Sad Page."

A title of no mean poetical worth—as indeed most of the titles in this picture can be described—introduces a sequence bold in its approach and execution and extraordinarily moving and horrifying in its effect. "The torch of war against the breast of Atlanta," "The Bombardment and the Flight," are the titles and the scenes themselves, some of them double exposures with action in the immediate foreground and other scenes going on in another plane, as it were, of the frame, are of burning fires, people rushing to and fro, scenes that create a rhythm and hysteria unequalled in its time. Short shots, some lasting less than three seconds, all contribute to a sequence showing the horror and panic of warfare, during which the second Cameron son is wounded and dies.

The trenches of the Confederate troops

The title, "The Last Grey Days of the Confederacy," which carries its own irony, preceeds scenes showing the appalling conditions of the troops, "Parched corn their only rations." We learn eventually that the Little Colonel is to lead a charge. Long, sweeping panoramas, intercut with brief close-shots of the soldiers in the trenches builds up the atmosphere and tension before the charge. "The entrenchments separated by only a few feet" (title).

A wide panorama of the battle in progress

Almost thirty individual shots precede the actual charge, and when the charge begins, Griffith's camera becomes, as it were, one of the soldiers, moving swiftly alongside the Little Colonel. But Griffith does more than simply to involve us with the charge, which in itself can present no moral standpoint on the part of the director. A long shot from above the charge acts as a bridge to the Cameron family, grouped formally as if for a family potrait—but minus their sons—reading from the family Bible. Such a cut-back is startling in its effect but is not unusual for Griffith at this time. Such a device can be seen in his ABs five years previously. It can be imagined what effect a scene such as this, with no perceptible movement, intercut suddenly into a sequence of great movement and of building momentum, can have had on audiences in 1915. Of course, it was Griffith's intention to break the rhythm—in fact one could argue that he created the rhythm *in order* to break it—so as to bring his message across the more forcibly.

*Phil Stoneman helps the wounded Little
Colonel into the Unionist trenches*

The Little Colonel is successful in taking two lines of entrenchments, but, as the title puts it, "Only a remnant of his regiment remains to continue the advance." There follows a scene in which Ben gives aid to an enemy soldier lying in No Man's Land, between Ben's captured trench and the enemy lines, in which Phil Stoneman stands in command of a company.

In the last charge, Ben himself is wounded, but carries the flag to the Unionist lines himself and rams it into one of their cannon before collapsing. The title, "In the red land of death others take their places and the battle goes on into the night," follows scenes of fighting, and then the title "WAR'S PEACE" is followed by the dead bodies of both sides, and this shot is repeated in slightly different versions after wide shots of the fighting still going on.

The war over, Ben is committed to a military hospital in Washington, and finds to his great joy that Elsie Stoneman is nursing in that very

21

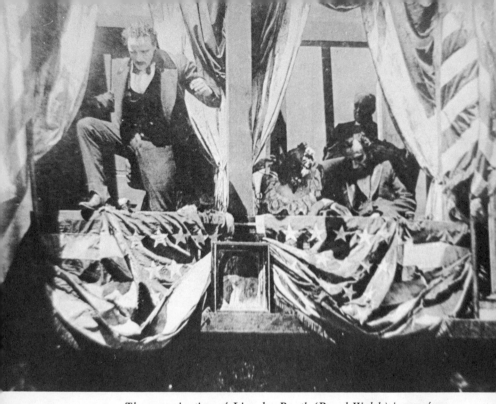

The assassination of Lincoln: Booth (Raoul Walsh) jumps from the box as Lincoln (Joseph Henabery) slumps in his chair

ward. Ben's mother visits him, and is horrified to learn that he is sentenced to execution as a guerilla. Elsie is as distressed as Ben's mother at this news, and exercises all her powers in obtaining an audience with Lincoln himself, seeking a pardon. As Ben's mother talks to Lincoln, the scene dissolves through to Ben himself in his hospital bed, and back again to the White House, and Lincoln eventually signs the pardon.

On the same day that General Robert E. Lee surrenders formally to General U. S. Grant, Ben Cameron is discharged, and his return home is probably one of the most familiar passages in *The Birth of a Nation*. The scene consists basically of two shots, and the first shot runs almost a full minute in length, which is extremely long considering the lack of action. This shot begins with Flora running out to meet Ben, whom she hasn't seen for several years. They look at each other for a considerable time, saying and doing nothing. Ben hasn't seen her since she was a child; suddenly, it seems, she is a woman. She remarks on his dirty uniform, he on her pathetic attempts to "dress up" by marking lumps of cotton with coal dust to produce "Southern Ermine." She then notices a bullet hole in his hat. They both pause to reflect on the past few years—and the horror of war, the disaster of its aftermath touches them both with shocking reality. Suddenly she breaks into tears and they embrace, Ben gently kissing her hair. They turn towards the door, the shot changes to a medium close-up of the porch, and from within the open door comes Ben's mother's arm, motioning him in, enfolding him, welcoming him home after the war. It is indeed a wonderful piece of cinematic understatement.

The title, "The Radical leader's protest against Lincoln's policy of clemency for the South," referring to Stoneman, heralds the general theme of racial unrest that is to dominate the rest of the film. Stoneman argues with Lincoln that the South should be treated as conquered territory, but, as the title puts it, "The South under Lincoln's fostering hand goes to work to rebuild itself."

But this determined attempt on the part of the South is destroyed completely by the assassination of Lincoln. When this news reaches Piedmont, Ben's family is plunged into the deepest gloom: "Our last friend is gone. What is to happen to us now!" On that pessimistic note, with Ben and his father already sensing the answer but not daring to utter it, the first part of *The Birth of a Nation* comes to an end.

*   *   *

The second part of this gigantic picture carries the sub-title "Reconstruction" and deals in the main with the racial strife that followed the Civil War and the Nation's loss of its liberal champion Abraham Lincoln. It deals, and was severely criticised for so doing, with "The agony which the South endured that a Nation might be born" (title). The action is preceded by a full two minutes of introductory titles.

These titles in the main quote Woodrow Wilson, in his "History of the American People." The passages quoted set the scene for the action that follows by putting into a nutshell the political ambition of Stoneman, which is essentially to *"Put the white South under the heel of the black South"* (title).

Stoneman introduces his *protégé,* Silas Lynch, a mulatto whom he determines to set as an example to all coloured people. "The blacks," he declares, angrily telling Lynch not to scrape to him or anyone else, "shall be raised to full equality with the whites." But Stoneman falls ill, and is obliged to send Lynch to the South in order "To aid the carpetbaggers in organising and wielding the power of the Negro vote." As Lynch is leaving, he sees Elsie, and his glance speaks volumes. His newly-found emancipation is already turning against the wishes of his benefactor.

Stoneman himself arrives in Piedmont soon after, "influenced by his children" to stay in "the hometown of the Camerons." Stoneman introduces Lynch to Ben, who refuses to shake hands after a brief encounter earlier in the day in which Lynch had shown his rudeness to the Cameron girls. A title then makes explicit the mulatto's own ambitions:

> "Lynch a traitor to his white patron and a greater traitor to his own people, whom he plans to lead by an evil way to build himself a throne of vaulting power."

The election is carried by the Negroes, while the whites are disfranchised. Lynch becomes Lieutenant-Governor and, as the title puts it, "Encouraged by Stoneman's radical doctrines, Lynch's love looks high." He looks again, longingly, but, it must be said, not without a certain archetypal evil grin, at Elsie.

Back at Cameron Hall, Ben is telling a group of friends about incidents involving whites and blacks which have seemed to him unjust, and these incidents are shown as flashbacks, while Ben continues relating them. Even as he talks, we see his own servant being flogged for not voting with the Union League and Carpetbaggers.

The scene changes to a sequence that tries to set the film historically rather than adding anything to the development of the narrative. "The

24

Negro party in control in the State House of Representatives, 101 blacks against 23 whites, session of 1871." Griffith goes to great lengths in a sub-title to establish the accuracy of this sequence, even quoting reference to a "Photograph by 'The Columbia State'."

The sequence on the surface gives the impression of the Negroes being unkempt, ill-mannered and boisterous. But we can see, to be fair to Griffith, that the general point being made is *political naïveté*, not racial characteristics. During this sequence, a bill is passed legalising intermarriage between the races.

A title draws the film down into the depths of gloom: "Later—The grim reaping begins."

The film returns to its narrative line and the following scene takes as its springboard the Bill passed in the previous sequence. Flora and Elsie are tailed by Gus, a Negro soldier. He never lets them see him, but unfortunately Ben spots him, and tells him to keep away from the girls. Lynch appears on the scene and demands an explanation from Gus. When Gus relates a story of ill-treatment from Ben he is furious and motions that "If he annoys you again I'll see that he learns his lesson." Ben goes indoors, "In agony of soul over the degradation and ruin of his people" (title).

Ben wanders along the river, desperate. He sees some Negro children playing with two white children. The two white children hide beneath a sheet and the Negroes run off terrified. A title follows: "The Inspiration"

> "The result:
> The Ku Klux Klan, the organisation that saved the South from the anarchy of Black rule, but not without the shedding of more blood than at Gettysburg, according to Judge Tourgee of the Carpetbaggers."

The first sortie of the Klan sets out to terrorise a Negro disturber and barn-burner. But Lynch scores first blood and in an ambush kills two of the horsemen. When Lynch then presents the costumes to Stoneman, the enraged Senator proclaims, "We shall crush the white South under the heel of the black South!" Lynch leaves and Elsie comes in, only to be confronted with evidence from her father that her sweetheart is involved in the Klan. Elsie says that she will talk to him.

25

Henry B. Walthall explains to Mae Marsh "The Inspiration"

At their next meeting Ben accidentally lets his costume fall from beneath his coat, and although Elsie had already resolved to end their engagement, this confirmation of her doubts shocks her. But, she assures Ben, "You need not fear that I will betray you." She then leaves him and eleven shots, alternatively showing Elsie alone in her bedroom, and Ben, discuss in visual terms the emotional state of them both.

After a shot of Elsie sitting on her bed reflectively, there follows a long sequence (over one hundred individual scenes and lasting seven and a half minutes) in which Flora jumps to her death in a ravine after

Ben Cameron finds the body of his sister (right)

being chased by the Negro Gus. Perhaps the finest part of this sequence is the last part, for in three shots Griffith establishes once and for all the strong emotions which lead eventually to the "retaliation" of the KKK on the Negro militants. A beautiful and tender sequence follows, showing Ben finding the broken body of his young sister, carrying her home and the reaction of the family. We also see the Negro servants, still faithful to old Cameron, with the title, "And none grieved more than these." It is interesting how this scene, which to many represents one of the distasteful elements in the picture, compares with the original passage in Dixon's *The Clansman*. In the book, Flora is raped by Gus, and her mother decides the only honourable course, for themselves and the family "name" is to commit a double suicide. They therefore both throw themselves purposefully from the cliff into the ravine. It is an

Retaliation: Gus (Walter Long) is killed and left on Lynch's doorstep (George Siegmann in top hat as Lynch)

unpleasant passage and it does show how Griffith tried to soften the more blatantly racist passages in Dixon's book.

Gus, terrified at what is inevitably to become of him as a result of his passion for the young white girl, hides in a local gin-mill. But, after a violent fight, he is brought to trial before the Klan, and, after the predictable result, his body is thrown at the door of Lynch's headquarters, bearing a skull and cross-bones with the legend KKK scrawled on a piece of paper.

It is decided that the Klan should issue a summons to all counties that its members are to "Disarm all blacks that night." But Lynch's spies see Margaret Cameron with a KKK costume and Lynch "Hopes at last to wreak vengeance on Cameron House." The Doctor is arrested and taken away, but his faithful servants effect a rescue by posing

Dr. Cameron (Spottiswoode Aiken) arrested. (Robert Harron in an "extra" role can be seen second from right)

as mockers along with the other Negroes. After overpowering the guards, Phil Stoneman helps in the rescue, but manages to shoot a Negro in so doing. The Camerons and Phil take flight chased by Negroes, and their wagon breaks up in a ditch. They run for the shelter of a small cabin, in which two old soldiers live. The following title is nearly always met with derisive laughter by today's audiences: "The former enemies of North and South are united again in common defence of their Aryan birthright."

Back in Piedmont, Elsie finds herself along with Lynch and discovers his designs upon her when he proposes marriage. When she refuses, he pulls her to the window. "See!" he says in a title, "My people fill the streets. With them I will build a black empire and you as my queen shall sit at my side." Despite her refusals and demands to be allowed out of the house, "Lynch, drunk with wine and power, orders his henchmen to hurry preparations for a forced marriage." Predictably, as a result of the constant badgering and rough handling, Elsie falls into a faint. Lynch catches her in his arms just as Stoneman arrives. With orders to guard her carefully, Lynch leaves her with some of his guards and goes to see Stoneman, telling him that he wants to marry a white woman. Stoneman pats him on the shoulder, apparently saying "Good, good, well done my boy!"

Griffith now cuts back to the Klans assembling, several hundred riders starting off to their various appointed missions. This is followed by a reminder of the plight of the Camerons in the cabin. The scene again shifts back to Stoneman and Lynch. Lynch tells Stoneman whom he wishes to marry, and naturally Stoneman flies into a fit of rage. Elsie, who has managed to break free from her guard, smashes a window and cries for help. Two KKK spies hear her yelling and ride off out of town to fetch aid. Lynch is determined to get his way and is slowly becoming more and more violent with Stoneman as he insists that Elsie is to be his bride.

At the cabin, the Negro soldiers have arrived and shooting begins. The following sequence of shots is interesting because it is from this point that Griffith begins to build the tension of the closing stages of the picture by intercutting from one set of circumstances to another, and is a direct progression from the experiments with intercutting he made six years earlier at Biograph and which he refined throughout his

Elsie (Lillian Gish) screams for help

stay there and which can be seen here in a similar form as it was used
in *The Battle at Elderbush Gulch* two years earlier and as a predecessor
of the highly sophisticated approach to the technique employed in
Intolerance.

After a shot of the Klansmen riding along a road, there is a shot of
Elsie, bound and gagged. This in turn is followed by a family group,
absolutely static and formally grouped, looking through a window and
obviously distressed. We see what they are watching; rioting in the
streets. The sequence is repeated; family group, rioting in the streets.
Another family group and then a title: "Ku Klux sympathisers, victims

The Klansmen ride out

of the black mobs." A shot of men being hit in the streets, then being tarred and feathered, and then a shot of another family group, is followed by more rioting in the streets. A long-shot of the Klan riding across the screen introduces a third element again; the mob in the street is followed by a medium-shot of Ben and another rider. The street and the mob again, but this time the Klan ride into the town from the rear. There is confusion, and shooting. Inside Lynch's headquarters, a soldier comes rushing in and tells Lynch what is going on outside. Lynch tells the soldier to guard Stoneman.

Griffith now cuts back to the cabin, with a shot of Margaret Cameron remaining stoical as she has been throughout the picture, amid all the shooting. We return to Piedmont and the battle in the street briefly before cutting back to the cabin as five Klansmen arrive. Three are shot by the Negro soldier, but two escape and ride off to fetch reinforcements. Back in Piedmont. The battle is still raging in the street. Griffith now takes us back to Elsie and her father. Stoneman tries to leave but his guard prevents him. Elsie's guard leaves, and she immediately ungags herself but as she turns to run out is confronted by Lynch who has come in from behind. He picks her up and carries her through to Stoneman. His guards rush in to tell him that the Negroes are retreating outside, and at that moment several Klansmen storm in, and Ben reveals himself to Elsie.

Two shots of the besieged cabin are followed by the title "News of the danger to the little party," and the two Klansmen who escaped from the cabin rush into Lynch's headquarters and tell Ben. Ben gives his orders quickly, and goes out to liberate the cabin.

The scene shifts once again to the cabin, as the soldiers begin to close in. There are eleven shots in this one sequence at the cabin, and in total they run only twenty-eight seconds. It is worth casting our memory back to the scene of Ben's return home from Washington, with no action,

Henry B. Walthall reveals his identity to Lillian Gish

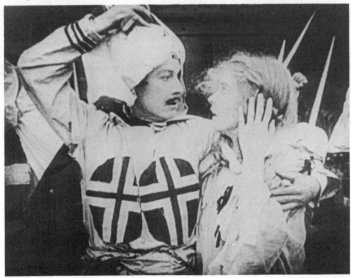

Victory Parade: Miriam Cooper, Lillian Gish and Henry B. Walthall in KKK uniform. In background Elmer Clifton as Phil Stoneman and Spottiswoode Aiken.

lasting a full minute. Here, with wild action, shots follow each other at a rate of under three seconds each. After those quick shots comes a shot of the Klan riding to the rescue. This single shot, lasting almost eight seconds, is followed by yet another sequence at the cabin, this time a group of fourteen shots and an overall running time of forty-three seconds. Another shot of the Klan, and again the cabin, but this time only four shots. The Klan again, and now only a single shot of the cabin. A tracking shot, or moving shot taken from a car, of the Klan precedes seven more shots of the cabin, at the end of which the Klansmen ride into view. After a short fight, the cabin is relieved.

This breathless sequence of shots is followed by a kind of epilogue to the film, in which the Negroes are disarmed and an uneasy order is restored. But, as we see in the next election when the Negroes are once again barred, there has been no progress towards any form of unity.

In *The Birth of a Nation* as in *Intolerance* which followed it, the film closes with allegory. After shots of Margaret and Phil and Elsie and Ben on a double honeymoon, the title "Dare we dream of a golden day when the bestial war shall rule no more. But instead—the gentle Prince in the hall of Brotherly Love in the City of Peace" is followed by a symbolical scene in which a god of war is raging on the back of a lumbering beast. This scene fades to be replaced by a scene in which the figure of Christ fades into the upper part of the screen.

A shot of Ben and Elsie on a cliff top makes a visual bridge to further allegorical scenes, in which people, singing and jubilant in the foreground, gradually fade away leaving a vision of a city in the background. Ben and Elsie, with the symbolical city superimposed in the sky above them, clasp hands and turn towards each other. The scene fades and the last title fades up: *"Liberty and Union,* one and inseparable, *now and forever."* This title eventually fades out.

The main title, *The Birth of a Nation,* including the words "The End" and copyright insignia and so on, follows, and it is this title that concludes the picture.

3. Intolerance

THE FOREGOING CHAPTER contains in essence the dramatic structure and internal construction of Griffith's first major work. Although Griffith's lasting reputation as the cinema's first important—and subsequently influential—figure has been built largely upon *The Birth of a Nation,* it is nevertheless true to say that he was still experimenting in this picture, just as he had been doing for the previous seven years. It is therefore still what might be termed a "formative" picture, in much the same way as for example *Judith of Bethulia, The Battle at Elderbush Gulch* and *The Massacre* had been before it, although admittedly on a much more grandiose and confident level. While this is true, it is also important not to forget that the character of Griffith was such that he never stopped experimenting, and indeed even after he had finished with film-making the years before his death were amply filled with drafts of new ideas, not only for motion pictures but also plays and material for other media, in which his passion for the epic was given ample scope.

However, although we have seen in the previous chapter how Griffith had broken free of all limitations of length and scale of motion pictures in which he was involved and had begun using all the techniques available to him to best possible advantage, it was in his next picture that all this knowledge and experiment was to be collated and arranged to produce a work which can truly be said to be that of a mature artist. Here, in *Intolerance* we see for the first time Griffith's supreme confidence in what he was doing, and his bold approach to narrative structure, and that genuine artistic quality of producing an idea and expanding it, extending it, building upon it and giving it sound construction and a richness of texture which only the most fertile of creative minds have been able to achieve on film.

In this volume, I have devoted a disproportionate amount of space to *Intolerance;* the reasons are twofold. Firstly, as already mentioned above, this film is Griffith's first really mature work, although *The Birth of a Nation* before it had been such a thorough training-ground for those who were to be involved in it, and also *The Birth of a Nation* had demon-

A production still from The Birth of a Nation *showing Sherman's march to the sea*

strated so perfectly Griffith's (and, for that matter, the cinema's) potential that the Civil War picture had tended to overshadow the greater achievements of *Intolerance*. Even today, the fact that *The Birth of a Nation* was such a water-shed in cinema history has understandably thrown *Intolerance* into a secondary place. Also, because of its somewhat inflammatory subject-matter, *The Birth of a Nation* has not unnaturally attracted far more attention than the no less passionate plea for tolerance which followed.

The second reason for such a lengthy look at *Intolerance* has a more direct bearing on the book as a whole and in some measure is responsible for the title of this volume. Already mentioned briefly is the glimpse that *The Birth of a Nation* gave the world of the potential of motion pictures; in fact to the press of the time it was more than a glimpse, it was the definitive demonstration of the power of the cinema: "I am thankful to have lived long enough to have witnessed this marvellous achievement in theatricals," said one critic, "to me *The Birth of a Nation* is the supreme wonder of the period." Another contemporary review said as a result of this picture that ". . . . the art of the motion picture is here, leaping forward as nothing artistic ever leaped before." "What could the stage give to rival this?" asked another stunned feature writer in 1915, "What the novel? What the poem? Nothing—everything else, music, poetry, song, depreciate into nothingness in comparison with such a marvellous portrayal of life and honor and patriotism." The film critic of the *Boston American* declared that "The spectator is almost lifted out of his seat by the passion and intensity of some of the scenes . . ." All this gives us a good impression of the critical climate of the period, and the one in which *Intolerance* was expected to overwhelm the impact of its predecessor. It hardly needs repeating that, predictably, the picture failed to do this to any lasting effect.

It failed, that is to say, to impress the public, to whom after all it was primarily directed. But the motion picture industry itself had already woken up with a start after the Civil War picture and naturally it saw the cinematographic virtues of *Intolerance* to even better advantage because of it.

The following chapter hopes to convey the complexity of the film, and it should be possible to see how it demonstrated in so masterly a fashion just how effectively the medium of pictures could be manipulated to convey not only passionate and emotional scenes but profound philosophical ideas and even abstractions and intangibles through basically *technical* considerations; arrangement and construction of narrative elements and the careful and deliberate employment of photographic techniques. These things brought home to an industry which had settled back in complacent confidence in one and two reel dramas or comedies that the industry, already over a decade old at that time, had only just begun its development. Things had to go forward, and Griffith was the man who led them.

Because of its technical expertise (as one consideration), *Intolerance* can be seen to have influenced the motion picture industry far more profoundly than had its predecessor, although the influence of *The Birth of a Nation* can be seen to be far-reaching and Seymour Stern claims that most spectacles immediately following its production and even including such recent productions as King Vidor's *War and Peace* owe their inception to Griffith's Civil War film. Be this as it may, the immediate effect *Intolerance* had upon the industry is far more obvious. On a superficial level it gave rise to many imitations, which failed to grasp fully the one quality which made *Intolerance* the masterpiece that it is, and among these imitations was Thomas Ince's *Civilization* which never approached Griffith's film either in depth nor technical complexity, although Ince's pretensions were undoubtedly well-meaning. *Intolerance* contains so many elements, as will be demonstrated, and these are all successfully blended into an integral and dramatic whole. Other filmmakers found enough in one reel of Griffith's picture to provide them with material for the basis of many subsequent productions, and Sergei Eisenstein for one acknowledged an everlasting debt to this picture which gave him his first demonstration of the language of the cinema. The sets of *Intolerance* remained standing in Hollywood far into the Twenties, emphasising once more the lasting impression that this picture had on the development of the American film industry, if not on the movie-going public in general. *Intolerance* can, I believe, be said to be at the root of the Rise of Hollywood.

*   *   *

David Wark Griffith's single-mindedness, the cause of his eventual downfall, both artistically and financially, at this time ensured that above all *Intolerance* would be a work of singular unity of style, a factor which

Constance Talmadge

Mae Marsh

Lillian Gish

Miriam Cooper

in hands other than Griffith's might be more than somewhat doubtful. There have been many superlatives used to describe this picture, and these all add up to confirm the film's undeniable place in the history of the cinema, and indeed to Griffith's stature as one of its first and greatest artists. Much has been made, for example, of the production costs, the amount of extras employed in this shot or that one, the dimensions of a particular set or the time it took to complete the film, and so on. But for my purposes I propose to examine the film itself—rather than its history—at least in some detail, in an attempt to analyse the mechanics of the picture, and also, because this is inevitably the result of these mechanics, the emotional charge that the film generates. Although the size and magnificence of *Intolerance* obviously depended originally on the statistics now legendary in film history, it is in the end the picture itself which matters; the action that passes before us on the screen and the message of love and tolerance that the film impresses upon us.

Griffith's angry response to the critics and censors of *The Birth of a Nation* first took the form of a pamphlet, entitled *The Rise and Fall of Free Speech in America.* In this, he condemned all forms of censorship and asserted his right to present things as he saw them and in his chosen medium. The word "Intolerance" runs all through it, and, showman that Griffith always was, it cannot have been merely coincidence that the word was to be the title of his forthcoming film; indeed, the pamphlet would provide some healthy publicity, as well as providing Griffith with a defence of his artistic integrity, for his next, and greatest, motion picture. There are clues in the text itself that further this suspicion:

> "The reason for the slapstick and the worst that is in pictures, is censorship. Let those who tell us to uplift our art, invest money in the production of an historic play of the time of Christ. They will find this cannot be staged without incurring the wrath of a certain part of our people. The Massacre of St. Bartholomew, if produced, will tread upon the toes of another part of our people."[3]

In this way Griffith was not only upbraiding his critics of *The Birth of a Nation,* but also, in a sense, almost dared them to criticise *Intolerance* which in itself was to be Griffith's own testament against those who would have censored his previous, and, in Griffith's own view, perfectly honest, work.

Griffith had already completed *The Mother and The Law* by the time that *The Birth of a Nation* was released early in 1915. This film, as we shall see, was to become the nucleus of *Intolerance*. But the total production period for the whole film was over twenty months and the editing of the picture occupied a further two months, at the end of which time Griffith, emotionally and creatively exhausted, must have felt his greatest work had been achieved. In this light, his statement that it was to be his last picture gains credence, although his own published reason (*Photoplay,* November 1916) falls in line with his pamphlet and the philosophy behind the picture itself:

> H. S. Gordon: "Is this truly your last picture?"
> Griffith: "It is—intolerance that I have met with and fought with in my other picture (*The Birth of a Nation*) makes it impossible for a real feature film, with the result dependent on the whim or lack of brains of a captain of police."

This last reference was presumably to the same captain of police Griffith mentions in his pamphlet: that of Chicago; Griffith found it ludicrous, although only to be expected, that "a man of the mental calibre of the captain of police of Chicago can tell two million American people what they shall and shall not go to see in the way of a moving picture."[3] Again, his assertion that *Intolerance* was to be his last work must have been largely due to his inborn sense of showmanship, for Griffith was far from drained of his filmic inspiration.

Intolerance begins and ends with the same image, whose simplicity cannot help but convey the link between—specifically—the four stories that follow, and—in a much wider sense—every action made by man; the link of mankind. The image is of a woman rocking a cradle. This is Griffith's central symbol, the common denominator, the cradle out of which the whole of mankind has grown. Harold Dunham traces the source of this idea:

> "It is said that some twelve to fifteen years before, Griffith was walking with Wilfred Lucas, when they were both working in a road show, when Lucas caught sight of a woman rocking a cradle, and reminded Griffith of Walt Whitman's lines from *Leaves of Grass*: 'Out of the Cradle endlessly rocking' and 'Endlessly rocks the cradle Uniter of Here and Hereafter.' "[4]

"Out of the cradle endlessly rocking"—Lillian Gish

The image has a timeless quality, quite apart from the fact that it is used with equal effectiveness to introduce each story in each period of history; there is no hint of any period of dress of the girl, nor with the shadowy figures—the three Fates—who stand nearby in the background. Towards the end of the film, when the actions of all four stories are nearing their respective climaxes, Griffith even uses this image *instead* of sub-titles, thus solving a problem—if only temporarily—that was never really surmounted throughout the period of silent pictures. Lillian Gish, who played this part, even then realised the profound significance of her role: "I am not in it in person, but my heart runs all through it—and it seems more to belong to me than all my other work put together."[5]

The first story to appear in *Intolerance* is the Modern Story. As previously mentioned, this was originally planned and filmed as a separate picture called *The Mother and the Law* and Griffith had almost completed it when he decided to incorporate it into a much bigger and expansive plea against intolerance of various kinds. This story, based on true events drawn from two contemporary sources,* deals mainly with social intolerance, the miscarriage of justice and class-hatred.

At first we see a group of ladies who, because of their self-realised inability to share the youthful enjoyment with which they find themselves surrounded, propose to dedicate themselves to the abolition of pleasure and diversion in the community in an attempt to reduce the people to their own idea of respectability. In order to make this effective, they need funds, and they approach Mary Jenkins, unmarried sister of a rich and influential industrialist. We see her at a party she is

* The Federal Industrial Commission, in an official report, cited a chemical factory combine, under the control of a man "fervid in charity and zealous in ecclesistical activities" whose practice it was to pour his companies' profits into charities while keeping his employees' wages at $1.60 a day. A request, subsequently refused, of a rise to $2.00 a day led to a full scale strike, which was brought to a halt only with the co-operation of "deputy sheriffs" and "constables" and at the cost of the lives of no less than nineteen of the strikers. The Steilow murder case, in which an innocent man was actually brought to the electric chair, provided Griffith with the germ of the second idea in the Modern Story of *Intolerance*. This incredible case includes the gruesome detail of the fact that the innocent man was reprieved only when being placed in the chair, his trouser leg already slit for the electrode.

giving, entertaining young men who continually prefer the company of girls their own age rather than Miss Jenkins herself. Her deeply-felt isolation from "the younger world" is indicative of the fact that she is about to become one of what Griffith calls "The Vestal Virgins of Uplift." Jenkins's Mill is the only source of employment in the small town, and most of the main characters at this stage are introduced through the mill. The Dear One's ageing father is employed there, and so too are the Boy and his father. When we first see the Dear One (Mae Marsh), she is playing among ducks, watching them waddle contentedly about, and recognising the simple attraction to each other that they

The strikers

share. Here again is Griffith's insistence on identifying his leading women with animals in the opening passages of a picture, in order to underline their childish innocence—an innocence which, more often than not, as a result of the following action, gives way to a fuller maturity and realisation of what hardships life can offer.

The "Vestal Virgins of Uplift" succeed in interesting Miss Jenkins in their project, and she approaches her brother for the funds they require. But even Jenkins finds it difficult to raise the amount of money his sister demands, and as a result orders a ten per cent cut in all wages at his mill. From now on we are to witness how the intolerance of a few individuals will spread and expand through the enormous sums supplied by Jenkins from a self-styled group of reformers to the grandiose and powerful "Jenkins Foundation" employing many people; and how this intolerance will lead to the corruption of those it seeks to reform.

As a result of the cut in wages, a strike follows, and the angry workers are subdued by the militia. At one point during this sequence showing the defenceless workers being fired upon by the military, we can discern painted on a fence behind the crowd the words "The Same Today as Yesterday." Film historian Seymour Stern has noted that "It is commonly accepted that Griffith conceived the basic idea for the story of *Intolerance* when he saw a billboard advertisement from a train window, travelling from California to New York for the *première* of *The Birth of a Nation*, bearing the words, 'The Same Today as Yesterday.'"

During the shooting, several men, including the Boy's father, are shot down. Griffith makes his point even more meaningful and poignant by cutting from a shot showing the Boy cradling his dead father in his arms to one of Jenkins sitting alone in his large and empty office. Griffith uses this shot of Jenkins several times during the film to give a scene added dramatic content.

And so the escalation continues. The Committee of seventeen, as the reformers now call themselves, drive many people jobless as a result of the strike from the town to a nearby city. The Boy, as a last and desperate resort, turns to theft in order to survive, while the Friendless One (Miriam Cooper), a one-time neighbour of the Boy (Bobby Harron), is taken into the employ of the Musketeer of the Slums. Before very long, the Boy, too, is drawn into the Musketeer's gang. The Dear

One and her ailing father are forced to live in a sordid slum, and gradually this brings about his eventual death.

Up to this point we have been presented with a ruthless picture of social intolerance and class-hatred, and it is one that will grow to frightening proportions later on. Griffith is never afraid to push home his point as far as it will go, and it is after this sequence in which we are shown the degradation of human morals and standards that a parallel with one of the other stories underlines the fundamental cause of this degradation. Immediately following the sequence in which the Dear One's father dies, we see first the shot mentioned above of Jenkins alone in his huge office, and then Griffith switches to the Judean story, equating the reformers of the Modern story with the Pharisees in the story of Christ. The Pharisees arrive at Cana just as the wedding feast is getting underway. There follows the sequence in which Christ performs the miracle of turning the water into wine, preceded by the title, put into the mouths of the Pharisees, "Meddlers then as now. There is too much pleasure-seeking among the people."

The construction of *Intolerance* is such that each story continually finds parallels with itself in one or more of the other three, is complemented by the other stories, and is made more forceful dramatically by comparison. There are many times when the narrative of one story stops abruptly to give way to another story; but the linking of the factor, either the image of the cradle or a more direct parallel in the action of the two stories, carries on the momentum of the film and the effect is almost never jumpy or irritating. Griffith chooses to make several parallels between the Pharisees and the Committee of seventeen. Apart from the one already mentioned above, he cuts from them to the Woman Taken in Adultery sequence from the Judean story: "He that is without sin among you, let him first cast a stone at her."

The Modern story and the Babylonian story all but force out the less-documented Judean and Medieval stories.* But this is not to say that these two seem in any way incomplete.

* Howard Gaye, who played the Nazarene in the Judean Story, claimed that the original print of *Intolerance* included some thirty episodes from this period. There remain only six episodes, apart from a few subtitles of quotations from the Bible. This is due, according to Howard Gaye, to the Jewish Authorities of Los Angeles, who insisted on the Judean Story being heavily cut at the time of the film's release.[6]

47

Christ at Cana: Howard Gaye as the Christ and Bessie Love (second from right) as the bride; George Walsh (extreme right) as the bridegroom

They both exist in a form that provides the perfect foil for the two dominant sections and naturally help to underline the theme common to all four stories. Of the four, the Modern story is the most detailed and telling against intolerance, because probably this is the closest to our own experience—the characters are perhaps more identifiable with, for example. The Babylonian story is the most spectacular, and it is on the basis of this, one suspects, that the film has earned a lot of its legendary fame.

Dealing primarily with religious and political intolerance, this story relates how Belshazzar manages to repel Cyrus, the leader of the invading Persian Army. He is eventually betrayed by the ambitious and jealous High Priest of Bel, and the city and its culture falls to the ravages of the invaders. Griffith again chooses to create a central character in the story whose role in the succeeding events is not a strategic one; that is, who has little or no control over her situation. He does not, for example, amplify the characters of Belshazzar or his Princess Beloved, who are to some extent the controllers of their own and their people's lives. It is they, at any rate, who are in a position to decide what should be done, what course of action should be taken in an emergency. Instead, Griffith introduces the character of the Mountain Girl (Constance Talmadge), whose brash unsentimentality fits particularly well into the story. She is a sort of *Hearts of the World* "Little Disturber" character, whose counterpart is Belshazzar's Princess Beloved as it was Lillian Gish in the war picture. In the process of the film, the Mountain Girl, as did the Little Disturber, will develop an affection for the man whose love is already sworn; in this case Belshazzar, as it was the Boy in *Hearts of the World*.

The Mountain Girl, as the Babylonian story begins, is being pestered by the Rhapsode, who is a "poet agent" of the Priest of Bel. A few light-hearted scenes of his attempt to attract her attention give way eventually to the main subject of the story. The High Priest of Bel, in an attempt to bring down the religious and social systems that Babylon enjoys and to replace them with his own ideas of government and worship, prays that the invading army of Cyrus, now approaching the city, will be victorious and will enable him to establish himself with the minimum of struggle in the throne of Belshazzar with the overthrow of the city. A title reads: "The jealous Priest of Bel sees in the enthronement of Ishtar loss of his religious power. He angrily resolves to reestablish his own god—incidentally himself."

The city proves too well fortified for the invading armies, however, and Cyrus is forced to retire after a long and spectacular battle. Harold Dunham, in his study of the careers of Robert Harron and Mae Marsh, gives some fascinating accounts of Griffith's efforts to achieve a high degree of realism in the battle scenes in *Intolerance*:

> "It is said that in the battle scenes Griffith had a brass band on
> the lot for three days playing suitable 'battle music' to en-

courage the efforts of the armies of extras. According to *Photoplay* of November 1916 the fighting men were trained to a high degree of ferocity, and became known as 'Griffith's Man-Killers.' Minor casualties were frequent, and on one day the ambulance is said to have been called 60 times."[4]

Throughout the battle we see the Mountain Girl, now in her suit of armour, fighting—not so much for the city as for Belshazzar himself—like any man against the Persian invaders. Her affection for Belshazzar is stirred first when she is taken to the Babylonian Court by her brother because he finds her too troublesome, and is promptly put up for sale on the marriage market—a courtyard where the nobles of Babylon choose their wives. Not altogether surprisingly, since she insists on eating raw onions, no one wishes to purchase her. Just then, the Prince Belshazzar himself enters and, after hearing her plaintive account of how she came to get there and how no one wants her for a wife, presents her with a seal which gives her the right to marry or not as she wishes. Naturally, Belshazzar never gives another thought to the girl after this incident, but she herself comes to idolise "her prince."

Griffith uses this scene in the marriage market to comment on modern-day methods of courtship. As the Mountain Girl ascends the steps to the platform to be viewed and assessed by the prospective husbands, he inserts the title "The Girl's turn—perhaps not so different from the modern way."—this is a sentiment that appears in the Modern Story, where he shows women parading like peacocks up and down the street in order to attract men. The Dear One herself, in her naïve way, attempts to mimic them, in the hope that then "maybe everyone will like me too." This scene of an innocent and ingenuous girl is directly preceded by a scene in which the Musketeer of the Slums embraces the Friendless One (who has since become his girl) with such passion as to give the Dear One's experiments added poignancy and meaning.

The Medieval story concerns the events immediately preceding the Massacre of St. Bartholomew's Day, 1572, when the Catholic religion in France finds itself responsible for the massacre of large numbers of Protestants, or Huguenots. Again, Griffith makes as the centre of the story a romance between two people whose lives will be affected by the

The Mountain Girl (Constance Talmadge) and doting Rhapsode (Elmer Clifton)

Imitation of the "fashionable" walk. Robert Harron and Mae Marsh

events although they themselves will have no control over their fate. In all four stories the predicament of the central characters is the same. They are ordinary people who are affected by the decisions and actions of, and conflicts between, those whose power leads them to intolerance. It is those in power of whom we see least, care least about, despise most.

At first we are introduced to those who by their decisions will affect the lives of the ordinary and helpless citizens. Catherine de Medici seeks to instigate the overthrow of the Protestant movement which at this time is beginning to gain considerable power against the Catholic majority. To do this, she needs to gain the consent and support of Charles IX, which she is in the process of doing as the Medieval story begins.

Charles is reluctant, being peace-loving by nature and also favouring the Huguenot elements in his court, but the Queen Mother Catherine is persistent. By the use of the sub-title, "Catherine de Medici, queen-mother who covers her political intolerance of the Huguenots beneath the cloak of the great Catholic Religion," Griffith ensured that he would not be accused of attacking Catholicism by emphasising that the massacre is engineered by *political* aspirations rather than religious ones. Indeed, it would be unlikely that he should, since both the Dear One and the Boy in the modern story are Catholics.

Before long the emphasis shifts from the magnificent court of Charles to the house of Brown Eyes, a Huguenot by religion, who is saying goodbye to her sweetheart Prosper. A very large close-up of Brown

Catherine de Medici (Josephine Crowell)
pesters Charles IX (Frank Bennett)

Brown Eyes (Marjorie Wilson) and Prosper (Eugene Pallette)

Eyes (Margery Wilson) conveys all the contentedness and tenderness of a young girl in love, and it is typical of Griffith to pour everything we need to know about a character into one long (almost six seconds) and revealing close-up of her face. Almost without realising it, faced with this shot we are able to place precisely her character and feelings.

But into this appealing idyll Griffith inserts a subtle presage of the tragedy that is to follow. As Brown Eyes says farewell to Prosper we see a mercenary soldier standing in the background, eyeing her lasciviously. When at last Prosper has gone, the soldier rushes up and grabs her by the arm, telling her how much he loves her. She shakes the mercenary off brusquely, and closes the door in his face. But already we have an idea of what is to follow; Griffith has given us a clue, in breaking up the purity of the situation by having this bearded, rough soldier force himself upon the simple and vulnerable girl.

As a result of the Dear One's attempts to attract attention to herself by imitating women in tight dresses with swaggering walks, the Boy is captivated by her charming innocence. "Say, kid, you're going to be my chicken" reads a sub-title during a scene in which the Dear One experiences the unforseen results of her experiment. The Boy runs his fingers along her arm, and she registers successively alarm, embarrassment and ecstasy—after which the Boy pulls her towards him and kisses her. Her father arrives, and hustles her upstairs, making her kneel before the statuette of the Virgin and "pray to be forgiven."

The Dear One's father, old and with a weak heart, finally dies through his "inability to meet new conditions." This scene, darkly lit with heavy shadows in the little apartment room, carries with it a great pathos and sense of grief that are due entirely to the forcefulness of Miss Marsh's acting. Mae Marsh wrote of this scene, which is not one that has attracted too much attention in this extraordinary film, at considerable length in her autobiography.

"While we were playing *Intolerance,* one cycle of which is still being relcased as *The Mother and the Law,* I had to do a scene where, in the big city's slums, my father dies. The night before I did this scene I went to the theater . . . . . . to see Marjorie Rambeau in *Kindling.* To my surprise and gratification she had to do a scene in this play that was somewhat similar to the one that I was scheduled to play in *Intolerance*: it made a deep impression on me.

"As a consequence, the next day before the cameras in the scene depicting my sorrow and misery at the death of my father, I began to cry with the memory of Marjorie Rambeau's part uppermost in my mind. I thought, however, that it had been done quite well, and was anxious to see it on the screen.

"I was in for very much of a surprise. A few of us gathered in the projection room and the camera began humming. I saw myself enter with a fair semblance of misery. But there was something about it that was not convincing.

"Mr. Griffith, who was clearly studying the action, finally turned in his seat and said—'I don't know what you were thinking about when you did that, but it is evident that it was not about the death of your father.'

" 'That is true,' I said. I did not admit what I was thinking about!

The Dear One converts the Boy: Mae Marsh and Robert Harron

"We began immediately on the scene again. This time I thought of the death of my own father and the big tragedy to our little home in Texas. I could recall the deep sorrow of my mother, my sisters, my brother and myself."[1]

When the Dear One's father dies, the Boy's genuine tears of sympathy reveal his true character, still retained under a veneer of lawlessness which he wears for the Musketeer of the Slums. Their subsequent courtship is complemented by that of Brown Eyes and Prosper, who, as Griffith explains in a sub-title, are "happily ignorant of the web Intolerance is weaving around them." The Dear One and the Boy are only too aware of their own predicament and the cause of their suffering, but they are powerless to control the situation as Brown Eyes herself. However, there follows a short interlude of happiness amongst all the misery inflicted by intolerance, with Brown Eyes and Prosper listening to her father reading. "Love's silent mystery" points the scene, which is followed by one showing the Dear One, whose "passing days of youth have healed the wound," and the Boy spending a "Coney Island day."

The Committee of seventeen, now calling itself the Jenkins Foundation, has meanwhile succeeded in purging the city of all drinking and dancing. After a sequence in which they congratulate themselves and we are shown the empty bars and dance halls turned into restaurants

The Boy leaves the Musketeer of the Slums (Walter Long) and demonstrates his strength to prove it. In the doorway Miriam Cooper

or simply deserted, Griffith then shows us where all the "pleasure-seeking" has gone. We see men distilling their own liquor in cellars and people dancing secretly behind buildings—an extraordinarily prophetic anticipation of the prohibition years incidentally. "When women cease to attract men they often turn to reform as a second choice" accompanies close-ups of members of the Foundation watching a raid on a brothel, a series which is followed by one close-up of an old and toothless man.

The Boy proposes to the Dear One, and they eventually marry. Such is the persuasive innocence of the Dear One that he is soon to realise the

"Intolerated away for a term"—Robert Harron

folly of his present existence. He tells the Musketeer of the Slums in no uncertain manner that he is giving up his life of crime, and he thrusts his pistol back into the Musketeer's hand. This is an action that is to become more significant than it appears, and the shot is repeated later on in flashback, for it is this gun that will condemn him to death. Ironically, his genuine self-reformation is to become his death sentence.

Frightened that this denial of allegiance is a potential danger to his own security, the Musketeer arranges a "frame-up" of the Boy by planting stolen goods on him after partially beating him up in the street. When the police arrive, the goods are discovered on him, he is arrested, and sent for a short term of imprisonment.

Griffith calls the penitentiary in a sub-title "The, sometimes, House of Intolerance," and people whose judgement is usually very sound and valuable have suggested that Griffith did this simply because he recognised that the Modern Story had in fact little to do with Intolerance. This is clearly not valid, since the central characters' lives are governed by the intolerance of the self-styled reformers. Their intolerance is as present in the Modern Story as in the Catholic hierarchy in the Medieval Story. To suggest that Griffith recognised a need to bolster up the Modern Story with obvious titles shows a remarkable lack of insight. One can find titles such as the one quoted above, or "Intolerants away for a term" in all four stories. In the Medieval Story for example, those who seek to instigate the massacres are called "the Intolerants," and the King despises what he calls "this intolerant measure." Again, in the Babylonian Story, Griffith calls Cyrus's sword of war "the most potent weapon forged in the flames of intolerance." Perhaps these titles may have dated after half a century, but this fact need not necessarily indicate that they replace an element in the film itself.

The battle between Cyrus and his army and Belshazzar is still after fifty years one of the most exciting and horrifying battle sequences ever filmed. Tinted red in the original printing, the impression of this passage must have been overwhelming, but even in monochrome, however, the battle reaches fever pitch and Griffith indulges himself in extremes of violence, every bit as harrowing as his extremes of sentimentality are placid. We see shots of soldiers gnawing at each others' throats and several soldiers being beheaded. Those shots in which men are impaled by the lances of their enemies are treated in such a deliberately horrific manner—not just as incidents of violence serving to continue the flow of action and maintain the tempo, devoid of any sense of the loss of human life—but so as to create a feeling of nausea in the spectator. And it is this effect which Griffith surely refers back to in the last images of the film, which are desperate pleas for peace and tolerance. Griffith uses the horrors of war, not for their sensationalism, but to turn us violently against what he depicts.

During the period of the Boy's imprisonment, his wife gives birth to their first child, and there follows a brief sequence typical of Griffith who depicted similar situations in several other works, in which we see the Dear One playing with the child and finding in her love for the infant a source of considerable solace amid the injustices that have so far befallen her. This sequence is directly preceded by the image of the cradle and the title, "Out of the cradle—endlessly rocking. Baby fingers hopefully lifted."

The now-powerful Jenkins Foundation hear of her case, and, in view of the fact that the husband is already branded a criminal and that she and the child live in a slum district, they decide that the child would be better off in their own clinic. They therefore make a call on the Dear One to verify the reports they have received. Before they arrive, however, we are shown her visiting a neighbour who gives her a bottle of whisky as a remedy for a slight cold. While she is out, the group from the Foundation arrive to find the baby unattended and assume expressions of an "I told you so" or "It's just what you'd expect" nature. The Dear One returns, whisky bottle in hand, and greets them in a friendly manner, not realising their ultimate purpose. The group see the bottle she is holding and before she is able to offer any kind of explanation they once again find their suspicions confirmed. They tell the Dear One that she is no fit mother, and she flies into an uncontrollable rage, chasing the women out of the room with a broomstick. The group go away, but, unknown to the Dear One, only in order to report and to obtain a warrant for the seizure of the child.

When they return some time later, the Dear One is in the middle of a modest meal, with which she is drinking a glass of beer. This naturally only helps to convince the group of the child's "undersirable" environment. The scene that follows is one of shattering dramatic intensity. One of the women tells the Dear One that they have come to

The Dear One protects her baby . . . (see over)

seize the child, and picks up the baby from its cot. The Dear One, stupefied, snatches the baby from her and backs away from the women, crying and screaming that no one will ever take her child from her. They fling themselves upon her and knock her to the ground, snatching the child from her arms and disappearing with it from the room, leaving

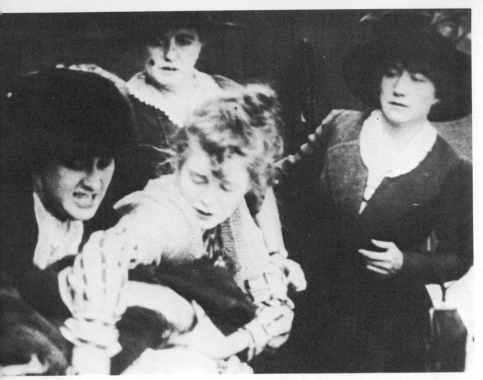

. . . but in vain—the Jenkins Foundation steps in

the exhausted girl half-conscious on the floor. Griffith shows us a close-up of the Dear One's head, and then pans slowly along her outstretched arm to reveal her hand lying across one of the child's bootees, perhaps stroking it in her half-conscious state.

The parallel Griffith draws here brings the sequence to a touching and poignant close. He cuts back to the Judean Story—without any linking title or images and superimposes over a picture of Christ surrounded by children the title: "Suffer little children."

Catherine de Medici continues to attempt to wrest from the distraught King the consent she needs to bring about the massacre of the Huguenots. She justifies her cause by quoting the Bible: "An Eye for an Eye" (a quotation that is to re-appear later on in the film), referring to the Michelade de Nîmes, which (not altogether made clear in the film itself) was an uprising by the Protestants against the Catholic majority some years previously, so named since it took place on St. Michael's day in Nîmes.

The battle between Cyrus and Belshazzar, lasting several days, at last ends in Cyrus's withdrawal and retreat, and a shot of the victorious Belshazzar embracing his Princess Beloved brings the first half of *Intolerance* to an end.

* * *

Griffith gave his film the sub-title, *Love's Struggle throughout the Ages,* and divided it into "a prologue and two acts." The prologue consists of all the action up to the death of the Dear One's father, and act two begins with the continuation of the Modern Story, with the Boy's release from prison and his reunion with his wife. This episode is linked directly (by the image of the Woman Who Rocks the Cradle) to the victory celebrations in Babylon.

The link between the Boy's return and Belshazzar's feast is not so slight or arbitrary as it might at first seem. In both cases the atmosphere is one of rejoicing and anticipation of more settled times ahead; and in both cases there is also a sense of loss—the Boy is confronted with the seizure of his child whom he has never seen—and in both cases also, the hope for the future is soon to be destroyed, quickly, and unexpectedly.

The feast itself is a scene of magnificent grandeur. It is this sequence that is most often quoted in textbooks; the set of Belshazzar's feast, over a mile in length and built to accommodate five thousand people without crowding. Bearing this in mind, it shows great restraint on the part of Griffith not to over-use the set. There are two long crane shots (that is, shots, beginning by being at a distance and a height above the set and gradually moving closer and descending to a group of dancers in the foreground) that accentuate the fabulous set, and then one or two shorter shots panning across the decorations on each side of the hall. It should be remembered that this set knew no precedent in the American cinema—nor for that matter in the whole history of

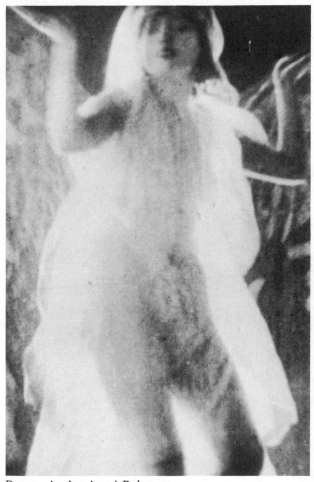

Dancers in the city of Babylon
Inside the Temple

65

Outside the Temple

moving pictures up to that time—and the temptation to linger on this scene at the expense of the narrative's tempo must have been considerable when we recall the cost of its erection and the number of extras employed for the sequence.

Belshazzar's feast reaches its climax—the people of Babylon imagine the defeated army of Cyrus miles away, presumably returning humbled to Persia, and the Prince orders a period of many days devoted entirely to drinking, dancing, and love-making. He promises his Princess Beloved that he will begin to build "her" city the very next day, and they both relax from the strains of war in the security of their mutual love.

The Mountain Girl is not allowed in the Great Hall where the main feast is taking place, but is content "in being even in the fringe of her hero's glory." Meanwhile, within the Hall itself, the festivities continue. We see Belshazzar's bodyguard—whom earlier we had seen decapitating enemy soldiers—playing gently with a dove (there is another important Griffith symbol—one that figures more than once in the course

"Kill them all!" Josephine Crowell and Frank Bennett

of the picture) and see half-naked girls, Virgins of the Sacred Fires of Life, dancing to the glory of Babylon.

But while Babylon rejoices, the High Priest of Bel has been putting into action his plan to betray the city to Cyrus the Persian, who, unknown to the Babylonians, is encamped with his forces not far from the city. The Priest instructs his agent, the Rhapsode, to ride out to the camp of Cyrus and inform him that the city is undefended and can be taken by storm and with little resistance. However, the Rhapsode, still seeking the favours of the Mountain Girl, hopes to win her over by boasting to her of this important mission with which he has been entrusted. The Mountain Girl disguises her horror by pretending she is impressed, so as to learn more of the betrayal of her hero Prince.

The preparations for the Massacre of the Huguenots goes on. Charles IX, at his wits' end, breaks down in the face of Catherine's persistence and consents to the massacre, yelling, "By God's death, since you wish it, kill them all! Kill them all! Let no one escape to upbraid me!" And

The Dear One's pathetic attempt to see her seized child

so the massacre is set in motion. Griffith returns to his central theme of helplessness in showing us Brown Eyes and her younger sister going to bed on the night of St. Bartholomew's eve. Outside, unknown to them, the mercenary soldiers are marking the house with white paint, showing that the inhabitants are Protestants.

When the Rhapsode rides out of Babylon on his mission of treachery, the Mountain Girl contrives to obtain a lift from one of his comrades and promptly disposes of him, before using the password the Rhapsode had confided with her to follow him out of the city.

It is at this point that the Musketeer of the Slums makes his reappearance in the development of the Modern Story. He ostensibly offers his help in getting the Dear One's baby back for her (this without the knowledge of the Boy) although in effect being as powerless as the Dear One herself. But his real motives are of a less genuine nature. His designs on the Dear One are suspected by the Friendless One, who follows him to her house, picking up, as she leaves, the gun that the Boy had thrown back at the Musketeer earlier in the film.

As it happens, when the Musketeer arrives, the Boy himself is out playing cards, and after first making sure that the Dear One is alone by looking through the keyhole, he knocks and she lets him in. A passer-by sees him go in, and, suspicious, rushes off to inform the Boy. Meanwhile the Friendless One arrives to overhear the dulcet tones of her unfaithful lover with the Dear One. The close-up of Miriam Cooper —who played this part—shows her biting her lip and drawing blood, trying to conceal the mental pain she suffers by self-inflicted physical pain.

When the passer-by arrives to tell the Boy of his wife's visitor, he can hardly get home quickly enough, suspecting the worst. As he comes up the stairs, the Friendless One, on the landing outside the door, quickly clambers out of a window on a narrow ledge. The Musketeer has by this time taken the Dear One roughly into his arms and is kissing her violently, despite her efforts to struggle free. The Boy bursts in, and a bitter fight follows, in which the Boy's strength is no match for the burly Musketeer. The Friendless One has meanwhile climbed along the ledge across to the Window into the Dear One's room. She draws the gun, and at this point Griffith fades the picture out and fades up a flashback, which is a repeat of an earlier scene at the beginning of

Intolerance, when the Boy, leaving the town after the strike, meets the Friendless One and offers to carry her bag. The scene fades out and Griffith once more returns to the Friendless One perched outside the window on the narrow ledge. She aims the revolver through the window and fires several times, fatally injuring the Musketeer before throwing the gun into the room and jumping from the ledge to the ground and escaping unnoticed.

In the room itself, all is confusion. The Boy picks up the gun without thinking what he is doing, utterly incredulous at what has happened. On the advice of neighbours, the police arrive and discover the Boy standing over the Musketeer's body, the murder weapon in his hand. He is discovered holding his own death-warrant.

This sequence is incredibly short. It is constructed in such a way as to convey each portion of the action, from the moment when the Musketeer leaves his house until his arrival of the police, as quickly and as precisely as possible. The whole passage lasts about five minutes, and contains one hundred and eleven shots averaging about three seconds in length. There is nothing at all to break up the action, which travels at a pace akin to that at which the characters themselves experience it. The effect is such as to create in our minds the bewilderment which is present in the mind of the Boy. And yet each action, the Friendless One leaving, putting the gun into her bag, the passer-by, the Boy playing cards, the Musketeer assaulting the girl, the movements of the Friendless One, all these shots are cut before the action contained within them is wholly completed, a device Griffith understood long before any other director of his era. Each shot is as brief as is possible without making it incomprehensible. For example, when the Musketeer leaves his house, the shot of his closing the door lasts for three-quarters of a second; of his going out into the street, just under a second; when he locks the door of the Dear One's room after being let in, the action of his doing so lasts, again, three-quarters of a second. When the Friendless One fires the revolver, the shot lasts only fourteen frames (and the film travels at sixteen frames per second). When she tosses the gun into the room, the shot of the gun landing on the floor lasts eleven frames; the following shot, of her leaping from the ledge, is exactly one second long. The next shot, of the Boy getting up from the floor, is ten frames long; the next, a continuation of the action of him rising, lasts only half a second. The sequence is over almost before we have realised what has happened, although in fact the whole passage is carefully and completely documented.

From this point onwards, the whole pace of the film quickens, and the events and the method by which they are presented to us on the screen generate, in the words of Iris Barry, "near hysteria."[2]

From the end of the above sequence, one shot of the Friendless One sitting nervously alone in her room leads straight into the scene of the Boy on trial for his life, facing a charge of murder and a penalty of death if found guilty. Griffith quite conventionally opens this, one of the most powerful sequences in *Intolerance,* by showing us a close-up of the Dear One as she shifts uneasily in her chair, watching the proceedings.

There follows a shot of the Friendless One—the real guilty party—whose actions are just as nervous. Next we see the Jury, and a fourth cut brings us to a shot of the Judge. There remains only one person's appearance to follow. The Boy himself is brought to the witness box, and is sworn in.

He is cross-examined by the council for the prosecution, and his guilt is practically established beyond questionable doubt. It *was* his gun; but his word that he had returned it is naturally discounted. Griffith inserts a flashback scene of the Boy giving the gun back to the Musketeer we saw earlier in the film. The Boy's defence council is totally ineffectual—it is his maiden case and he stutters helplessly in reply to the prosecution. The Jury therefore return a verdict of guilty. A sub-title, re-introducing the phrase "an Eye for an Eye" and developing the concept to "a murder for a murder," leads to a transition to the Judean story, where Griffith parallels the verdict with the Judgement of Christ; "Let Him be crucified."

The extreme close-up shots of the Dear One during her husband's trial are much quoted and illustrated as examples of Griffith's use of this technique in order to obtain dramatic intensity. Much more mention could be made, however, of the performance of Mae Marsh, which in this scene reaches one of its many peaks. Sir Alexander Korda included her performance as one of the most outstanding pieces of acting in the silent film era, and June Barry rated her playing of the Dear One as second only to Falconetti's Joan of Arc. But recalling Miss

Two close-ups of Mae Marsh during the courtroom scene

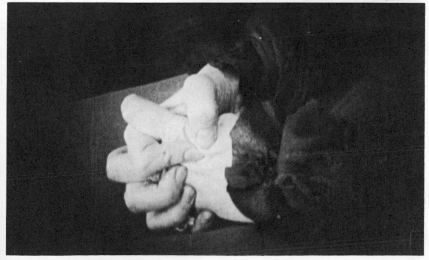

Marsh's youthful exuberance in the opening passages of *Intolerance,* her maturity to womanhood in these climactic scenes is one of the most natural transitions yet astonishing things Griffith has obtained from any of his actresses. She bears her grief to smile and wave nervously at her husband, suppressing the tears in case her husband should think her moral support is not forthcoming.

Miss Marsh herself, in her autobiography, has little to say about the scene, but there is little that words could add to the emotional force of her mime.

> "The hardest dramatic work I ever did was in the courtroom scene in *Intolerance.* We re-took those scenes on four different occasions. Each time I gave to the limit of my vitality and ability. I put everything into my portrayal that was in me. . . . Parts of the four 'takes'—some of them done at two weeks' intervals—were assembled to make up those scenes which you finally beheld on the screen."[1]

And speaking of the shots of her hands which appear in the scene, she goes on:

> "I quite unconsciously began to wring my handkerchief and press it to my face. 'Good,' he (Griffith) said, 'Keep it up'."[1]

Perhaps the phrase "Each time I gave to the limit of my vitality and ability," crystallises the intensity that surely no one seeing the film is unable to sense; the intensity that must be attributed above all to the ability of the actress or actor, but also in equal measure to Griffith himself, since, as Miss Marsh's statement implies, it was he who was able to coax from his players their utmost efforts. "He gave us," Miss Marsh has said, "of his genius and personality, and for that there is no return coin." Perhaps she did not altogether realise that in fact she had returned the coin already, in the form of the performance she gave him, and gave the world.

After the trial, when she has returned to her room, all the pent-up grief rises to the surface not, as might be expected, with much weeping and melodramatic gesticulating, but in one shot of Mae Marsh's drawn and incredulous face. She enters the room in long shot and walks slowly into full close-up, her face conveying all the deep and violent emotion of a woman's sensibilities in one eloquent portrait so typical of Griffith. No need here for mime or other substitutes for words; the motion picture camera has become, in the hands of D. W. Griffith, the true and unobtrusive mediator between the actress on the screen and the audience themselves, lifting her out of characterisation and into life.

And yet we are not to be spared the full extent of her suffering, because Griffith accentuates it with the cruellest of ironies. He follows this shot with a scene of Jenkins sipping tea with members of the Jenkins Foundation. The caption inserted reads: "The people everywhere are singing your praises."

A shot preceded by the title, "The irresistible impulse," shows the Friendless One returning to the scene of the murder, which in turn precedes a scene in which the Dear One discovers—with the aid of a neighbouring policeman—the method by which the Musketeer was shot—from a ledge outside the window. On her behalf, therefore, the policeman goes to the visiting Governor to make an appeal for the Boy's release. Again Griffith shows us the Friendless One, at home, playing solitaire, her conscience allowing her no respite. He then shows us her thoughts by introducing a shot of the Boy in prison. After a brief sequence showing him among the other prisoners, we learn that the appeal has been rejected, and the execution will go on as planned.

The treacherous mission of the Rhapsode nears its end as he arrives at the camp of Cyrus. We see the Mountain Girl watching the events from a distance, and the title, "The Great conspiracy" is followed by the Rhapsode delivering his message to the Persian leader.

The image of the cradle rocking brings us back to the Modern Story, where the title, "The Boy's last dawn" introduces a sequence showing the hangmen making their macabre preparations for the execution. The Dear One insists that they should try to appeal once more to the Governor, and the policeman, seeing her frantic state, cannot but agree. They do not realise, however, that they are being followed by the real guilty party, The Friendless One herself. They rush off to the Governor's hotel, and the Friendless One, her nagging conscience now almost unbearable, follows.

Brown Eyes, horrified, has a rude awakening from her childlike dreams—dreams, no doubt, full of romance and Prosper, her suitor. At this moment however, when the massacre of St. Bartholemew has already begun and Huguenots all over the city are being slain mercilessly, Prosper is out of Paris, and hears about the massacre long after its inception. Brown Eyes' father, realising at last what is happening, boards up his house and piles furniture behind the door.

The Dear One and the policeman arrive at the governor's hotel, as the Friendless One arrives soon afterwards, remaining some distance down the road, hoping she'll not be noticed. The Governor is just leaving for his train, and brushes off the policeman who is acting on the Dear One's behalf. He even ignores the desperate pleas of the Dear One herself. His decision, it seems, is final.

As the Governor's taxi draws away, the policeman and the Dear One stand stunned on the pavement. The policeman happens to look along the pavement and recognises the Friendless One, whom he had seen, presumably, at the Boy's trial. When she sees that she has been recognised, she begins to run for her taxi, but the policeman chases after her and catches her. The Dear One hurries after him and the Friendless One, at her wits' end, confesses that it was she who killed the Musketeer of the Slums.

Now there is no doubt about what to do. The chase, a standard device in silent movies and used extensively by Griffith to provide a thrilling climax to his pictures, is used again here. But it is given three times the emotional charge by virtue of the fact that while we are involved with the fate of the Boy, we are also concerned about the outcome of the other three stories, intermixed with each other. The Boy is to be hanged for a crime of which he is innocent, Christ is condemned to death for proclaiming himself the King of the Jews, the Huguenots are to be massacred because of their religion, and Babylon is to fall unless the Mountain Girl is able to bring the message to Belshazzar in time.

As the Dear One, the policeman and the Friendless One jump into the taxi and chase off to the station in a desperate effort to reach the Governor before he boards the train, The Mountain Girl, having watched the proceedings in Cyrus's camp, at last realises what is happening. Babylon, and "her prince," are being betrayed to the Persians. She jumps onto her chariot and races furiously back towards Babylon, closely followed by the whole Army of Cyrus.

The path to the scaffold: Robert Harron and a real
priest employed by Griffith for accuracy of detail

While the Boy is being given the Last Sacrament, the Dear One and
the guilty girl arrive at the station only to discover that the train has
already left, with the Governor on it. Suddenly all hope seems to have
disappeared. Then, the policeman sees a racing car in the station yard,
with a driver and his friends talking about the vehicle. The policeman,
followed by the two women, rushes over to them and explains his
situation. The driver does not hesitate. The policeman and the two
women crowd on to the car and the chase after the train begins.

A shot of the cradle leads directly into a brief sequence showing

the Mountain Girl approaching Babylon, minutes before the army which is about to ravage her city and its culture. This is followed, *without sub-title,* by a shot of the Boy's praying with the priest in his cell, which is in turn followed by shots of the racing car speeding after the train, travelling as fast as it will go, slowly overtaking it.

The massacre in Paris reaches its climax, with people being slaughtered in the streets. These scenes recall the violence and repugnance of the battle scenes in Babylon, with close-ups of blades entering men's chests, and blood spewing out. But amongst all this, there is one passage in which Griffith shows us even that "Intolerance, burning and slaying" retains a glimmer of humanity. A small child, terrified, falls at the feet of a Catholic priest. He takes her and hides her under his long cloak, and when soldiers rush into the picture after her, he points down the street, indicating that he saw a small child run off down it. The soldiers rush off in pursuit, and when they have disappeared the priest takes the child into his house.

The celebrations in Babylon are still in full swing, and Belshazzar plans the building of his Princess Beloved's new city ignorant of the dramatic race which is nearing the city. A title, "Cyrus sweeps on to Babylon's destruction," sums up the incredible shots of his massive army that follow it.

Prosper hears of the slaughtering of his people from a friend, and after gaining the badge of safety—a white armband—he rushes off to try and reach Brown Eyes. But even with the password, he is stopped and as a sub-title describes it, his "way is beset with danger." The mercenary soldier we had seen earlier on in the picture now makes his re-appearance at the house of Brown Eyes; the soldiers manage to break down the barricaded door. The father fires his gun, and kills outright the first few soldiers to enter the door. But there are many more behind, and before very long the whole household is wiped out. Only Brown Eyes, terrified child that she is, is left, and is approached by the soldier we saw when the story began, the soldier who told her he loved her so roughly, and whom she turned away and laughed at.

A shot of Prosper fighting his way through mercenary soldiers leads,

The dawning of St. Bartholomew's Day:
the massacre begins

through a shot of the cradle, to Christ hauling His cross through crowds of jeering people.

Shots of the army of Cyrus moving swiftly across the screen, and of chariots advancing rapidly towards the camera are followed, without any kind of transitional shot or sub-title, by a shot of the train, and a shot taken from a position very close to the wheels of the engine almost evokes the noise and clatter of the machine. Between this and the shots of the racing car speeding along in pursuit there is placed a shot of the Boy with the Priest. Griffith will not allow us to forget the reason for the chase and excitement. By inserting the shot of the Boy and the priest, he makes the chase more urgent, more vital, rather than slowing up the tempo of the action.

The image of the cradle rocking brings us back to the house of Brown Eyes, where the soldier has her at his sword's tip. He advances to her and takes her in his arms, but, unable to contain herself any longer, she faints in his arms. Prosper, hurrying to her rescue, is delayed everywhere, and has the utmost difficulty in persuading the soldiers that his password is genuine. Meanwhile the mercenary soldier is holding Brown Eyes in his arms, and loosens the thin nightdress she still wears before carrying her limp towards the bed.

Again the image of the rocking cradle makes the transition from one story to another, and this time we are brought back to the Modern story, where the racing car at last overtakes the train and succeeds in bringing it to a halt.

As the party dash from the car towards the train, the film switches without transition back to the Medieval story, where the soldier kisses Brown Eyes before killing her brutally by running her limp body through with his rapier. Catherine de Medici comes out from the castle to survey the effects of her massacre, and a shot of dead children, women and men is followed by a close-up of her face, partially hidden by a fan. She slowly lowers the fan to reveal a cold, hard smile on her lips.

Prosper arrives at Brown Eyes' house, only to find her body lying in a pool of blood. He picks up her body and staggers to the door, where soldiers prepare to shoot him. He yells hysterically, and the soldiers fire. He falls to the ground with the girl he was to marry, and embraces her lifeless body as he dies while a soldier passes in the background, carrying a pole, on the end of which is a human head.

This leads without transition to the last reel of the film, where the Mountain Girl at last reaches Babylon, but is delayed in getting to Belshazzar by the wine-crazed revellers. The image of the cradle rocking brings us back to the Dear One at last reaching the Governor and explaining about the Friendless One's confession. As he listens, Griffith again cuts back to the Boy in the cell being comforted by the Priest.

At last the Mountain Girl manages to gain admission to the Great Hall and to Belshazzar, who is annoyed by the intrusion of such an undesirable person. He listens to her however, but cannot bring himself to believe what he hears. At last, his own servants convince him as Cyrus and his troops surge into the city through the gates left open by the priests.

Babylon is soon overrun, and Belshazzar himself leads the resistance to the invaders; but the struggle is hopeless, and Belshazzar is enticed back to the city to commit suicide rather than suffer the humiliation of capture. And so, with his Princess Beloved, they both stab themselves through the heart, entering "the Death Halls of Allat" together. The Mountain Girl, courageous and loyal to the last, is hit by an arrow and dies. We see a close-up of her face, masked on the screen to occupy only the right-hand corner of it. The mask then pulls out to reveal the whole screen area, and we see two doves, doves used by the Princess Beloved as messengers of love when they carried messages from her to Belshazzar in a miniature chariot to which they were harnessed. The small chariot now is empty; the doves bewildered. The symbol of peace and love, amid desolation and slaughter.

The cradle rocking leads to the train pulling into a station; the Boy's pardon has been signed—all that remains is to reach the gallows before the trap-door is released. But the Boy is already being led to the gallows, and beside him still is the priest who, unable any longer to stand the strain, stumbles as he walks. Griffith cuts directly to a shot of Calvary Hill, and three crosses in the background, heavy swirling clouds overhead, and people in the foreground waving their arms to and fro.

The Friendly Policeman rushes to the nearest telephone to have the execution stopped. At the prison, a guard receives the call, and runs excitedly to tell the executioner, who is already supervising the preliminaries—the Boy is having a hood placed over his head, and the noose placed around his neck. Meanwhile the party have rushed to the prison in the car. They arrive outside the building as we see the noose being tightened around the Boy's neck, a shot which is followed by a shot of the executioners, holding their knives over the strings which will release the trapdoor.

Robert Harron is led to the scaffold

The Executioner is just about to give the signal when the Dear One, the Friendless One, the Governor and the Policeman waving the pardon excitedly in the air rush into the chamber, and the execution is stopped.

The reunion between the Boy and his wife is one of uncontrollable relief; and the woman he sees in his arms ruffles his hair, tears in her eyes, much as she played happily with ducks at the beginning of the film. But then she was a child; and now she is a woman.

This extraordinary film ends, as do most of Griffith's major films, on an optimistic note. And, as in *The Birth of a Nation,* the conclusion is one of apocalyptic visions, underlining the basic concept of the whole film in terms of its relevance to the whole of humanity.

A series of symbolic scenes, a battlefield with soldiers meeting in combat with bayonets, New York being destroyed by huge bombs, fantastic weapons of war and prisoners behind walls, are preceded by the title: "When cannon and prison bars wrought in the fire of intolerance . . . . . ." and give way eventually to shots in which rows of angels appear in the sky above the battlefields, arresting the soldiers in the act of killing. Beams of light stream down on the soldiers, frozen with their bayonets hovering above their foe. The title: "And perfect love shall bring peace forevermore," sums up the basis of Griffth's philosophy, and is followed by shots of the soldiers dropping their weapons. Following the third and last title of the film, "Instead of prison walls . . . bloom flowery fields," are shots of a huge prison, on which beams of light descend from the sky, and within the prison, the hundreds of prisoners rush forward towards the tall wall in front of them, which seems to disappear, allowing the prisoners to surge out to freedom. A shot of a large prison "dissolves" to a shot of an equally large field of tall grasses and flowers.

We see, finally, shots of children playing happily against a background of weapons of war overgrown with flowers. They are surrounded with people strolling about in brilliant sunshine. Two small children in the foreground make necklaces of flowers for each other, and the girl blows a kiss to the little boy, who in turn embraces her. They both laugh happily.

The film ends with the same image with which it began, the cradle, eternally rocking. The words "The End" fade up and the whole image fades to black.

*　　*　　*

We can see from the foregoing study of the narrative of *Intolerance* that the main source of excitement is the fact that there are four separate stories which all culminate in one paralleled climax, the climax that James Agee likened to "the swinging together of tremendous gongs."[7] But this is not the whole cause of the film's stature as a genuine work of art. Griffith understood certain principles of film editing and approaches to film-making which no other director of his time had yet had the courage to put into practice in a moving picture.

The effectiveness of this knowledge, as well as the effectiveness of the principles themselves, is more than evident in the film itself as it is in all of Griffith's pictures. When the film was first seen in the summer of 1916, it was barely understood by those who saw it, although the general reaction to it was one of overwhelming admiration for the mind that could conceive such a work. One Heywood Broun, writing in the New York *Tribune,* surely deserves some inverted distinction by having written in his article of October 20, 1916 that the bathing-beauty spectacle *Daughter of the Gods* "has the enormous advantage over *Intolerance* in that it tells a story." And this was not an unusual reaction to the film.

Edward Wagenknecht goes on:

> "If, as has been stated, spectators were confused by the woman out of *Leaves of Grass* who rocked the cradle marking the transition from one age to another, they must all have been mental defectives. John Howard Lawson says that nothing happened to her. What was supposed to happen to her? In a deeper sense everything that took place in the film happened to her, for all the characters were her children."[8]

Intolerance was a financial failure. The breadth of its vision and the manner of its presentation were too much for the audiences of 1916 to comprehend. They were bewildered; like Mr. Broun, they went to the movies to be told a story, in simple and readily understandable terms. Here, with *Intolerance,* they were presented with a film that asked them to think, to assimilate in their own minds rather than be presented with an easily comprehensible and simply constructed sequence of events. Griffith said of the film, "events are not set forth in their historical sequence, or according to accepted forms of dramatic construction, but as they might flash across a mind seeking to parallel the life of the different ages." But, alas, he underestimated his audience and as a result eventually lost his artistic independence. He was to pay the price for his boldness: even twenty years later when the film was revived in New York, *Variety* carried the following paragraph:

"... it proved too strong for many ... Dowagers especially
wilted under the bloody moments. In future when the film is
shown a warning may be posted beforehand, as catering only
to those with good stomachs, so as to offset any squawks ...
Elmo Lincoln's 'Man of Valour' characterization with its
head-chopping stunt caused the main yelp from the audience."

Towards the end of *Intolerance,* Griffiths cuts his shots to the absolute minimum length. Some last less than half a second, or eight
frames—and yet it is precisely this brevity of pictorial statement that
gives the film its pace, although in fact we hardly have time to register
the very existence of the shot. It is this technique, possibly rather than
the fact that he used the close-up to more dramatic effect than in any
of his contemporaries, that gives *Intolerance* its stunning visual momentum. Griffith is not interested in showing us events with a clinical
obsession for documentation: his world is one primarily concerned with
emotions, and his editing techniques are dictated wholly by the emotional content of the scene. This is not say, however, that full documentation of a particular scene is never found in Griffith's work: we
have already studied in detail the scene in which the Musketeer of the
Slums is shot, and have seen how Griffith was able to construct the
sequence with precise documentary accuracy and with a high degree of
emotional content as a result. This scene, as described earlier, has a
whirlwind effect on the senses; but Griffith was able, through his remarkable gift for directing actors and actresses, to generate an equal
amount of emotion on the screen through a simple and in many cases
stark setting, relying wholly on the skill of the player. Mae Marsh alone
in her room after the trial is a typical example. The actors and actresses
themselves, of course, would deny their own skill and credit Griffith
with the ability to "bring out" whatever it was that was their natural
ability. This is true of practically every actor or actress who ever worked
with him, and is a sentiment found in almost every published article by
a Griffith-trained player. The scene would always be his, not theirs.
James Agee admired this quality above all else in Griffith's work; "All
through his work there are images which are as impossible to forget,
once you have seen them, as some of the grandest and simplest passages
in music or poetry."[7]

Eisenstein, who admired and openly confessed his absolute debt to Griffith, saw the mechanics of *Intolerance* and could learn from them; he even lifted ideas. But he could not manipulate actors or actresses in the same way; and the difference of the two styles of film-making shows up very well the artistry of Griffith's players—which is to say it emphasises Griffith's directorial genius. In many minds, Griffith's use of technical devices—the close-up and so on—is the mainstay of his lasting reputation. But on closer analysis, and especially when his pictures are compared with those of the many directors who were his pupils, it emerges as a prime factor that where Griffith's technical prowess ends, his real genius begins.

Many of the actors and actresses in *Intolerance* left Griffith for long and illustrious careers ahead of them; Griffith had given them their inspiration and made of them actors of fine stature; actors who were capable of manipulation and sensible of the director's requirements. In 1917, the same year during which *Intolerance* was first seen, Griffith wrote, "For principals I must have people with souls, people who know and feel their parts, and who express every single feeling in the entire gamut of emotions with their muscles!"[11] And, in the same article, ". . . . some of the most widely advertised and most-admired spectacular pictures from abroad suffered from the defect of mediocre acting. Of what use are magnificent scenes with only puppet-like actors?"[11]

Griffith possessed an unusual flair for finding people—not necessarily trained actors—to work for him in his films, actors and actresses to whom he could communicate fully his needs for a particular scene.

He would demonstrate how the actress should play the scene, and the actress herself, more often than not moved (not by his performance—since this, according to contemporaries, was altogether atrocious in its melodrama—but his involvement in the situation depicted), would feel herself directly inspired by him. The scene in which the Friendless One (Miriam Cooper) listens outside the door to the Musketeer of the Slums seducing the Dear One, shows Miriam Cooper biting her lip and drawing blood. Bessie Love, who played the Bride of Cana in the Judean story, remembers in particular this incident during the making of *Intolerance*. She tells of the way in which Miriam Cooper was biting her lip with such realism as to create a real wound, self-inflicted by an actress who knew that Griffith expected of his actresses and actors all the passionate involvement he himself had in his work. All those people who worked with Mr. Griffith talk of him with the utmost respect and clearly everyone who acted under him was imbued with the same dedication. Bessie Love, in a recorded interview, talks in reverent tones of "his compassion, his understanding, his love of people. And of course he could make anyone on earth act. Nobody could have not acted with him. He was wonderful."

This illustrates vividly the kind of atmosphere in which *Intolerance* was made. And it goes a long way, too, towards giving an explanation of the sincerity with which everyone involved in the production approached their work.

This film, so gigantic and complex in its pretensions and yet so simple and basic in its approach, cannot help but create a lasting and deep impression on anyone who sees it. At times it achieves the intensity of a vision; one feels that the images on the screen have no recognisable counterpart in reality, so forcefully are they conveyed. And yet they *are* real, and so real that one can hear the screaming mass of hysterical crowds, the smell of blood, or the perfume of a young girl's hair. *Intolerance* shows, clearer than any other of Griffith's major works, his ability to construct large and spectacular scenes comparable only to a military manœuvre, alongside his equally powerful talent for lifting the simplest gesture, facial expression or the most basic and elementary of situations into the realms of the highest artistic achievement attained in the medium of motion pictures. This fact alone commands our respect of him as one of the most important of the figures in the development of cinematic art.

Griffith's method of staging the spectacular crowd scenes in *Intolerance* was to plant among his thousands of "extras" a selection of assistant directors whose job it was to excite the men and women around them into the hysterical state Griffith required. These assistants, many of them people who were later to become successful film directors in their own right, were instructed directly by Griffith himself, seated in a tower high above them and shouting directions through a megaphone. Albert Bigelow, quoting R. E. Long, comments:

> "The luncheon hour 'on location' composed one of the most
> picturesque sights ever witnessed by human eyes. At times

there were as many as fifteen thousand men, women, and children scattered over the various lots during the noon hour. Thousands of horses and sheep grazed along the green enclosures, their shaking heads mingling with the flashing swords and helmets of the fighting men.

When the great mob scenes were being photographed, it seemed as though the entire population of Los Angeles had come out to Griffith's place, to take part in the various pageants and mighty rushing armies. Actors from other studios—many of them prominent stars—joined the scenes."

But this fact alone is not the extent of Griffith's creative achievement. If it were, how dull those intimate scenes would be in which he is able to convey an emotional intensity worthy of a Goya painting; where it is necessary to think twice as to whether or not we metaphorically heard a cry, or a scream of terror, or a moan from the soul of humanity.

One laughs, for there is humour too in this picture. Belshazzar is told of the approach of Cyrus's army by his father, who enters to show Belshazzar an archeological "find" he has made: a brick laid 3,200 years before Babylon. Incidentally, and as an afterthought, he mentions that Cyrus is invading the city. Griffith never understood comedy in the sense that his contemporary and friend Mack Sennett understood it. Griffith's comedy is a gentle, human humour. His approach to the lighter side of life is apparent in the scenes such as those of the opening sequences of the Modern Story in *Intolerance,* where the Dear One plays and watches the ducks as they apparently "kiss" one another. His humour is touching; never cruel, never based on fear or on pain, and far from the slapstick basis of Sennett's films. Mae Marsh, as the Dear One, hops and skips in the sun when the Boy takes her for a day on Coney Island. She is happy; and her happiness shows itself in her awkward simplicity.

There is humour in each of the four stories. The Mountain Girl, in the Babylonian story, viciously slaps an innocent bystander whom she takes to be the man to have just kissed her on the neck, whereas in fact it had been the Rhapsode, who had crept up behind her while she was absorbed in watching Belshazzar, "her prince," pass by in a procession. In the Medieval story, it is Brown Eyes' small brother who provides the comedy by tantalising her and Prosper whilst they listen to her father reciting poetry. And again in that story there is the effeminate duke, fondling puppies in a pouch slung from his waist; a characterisation worthy of Stroheim.

Already mentioned are some comic elements in the Modern story. At the beginning of the Judean Story, it is established that the Pharisees demand that all action must cease when they decide to pray. Two of them appear—one of them played by Stroheim himself, incidentally—and begin their prayers. A close-up of an old man's munching an apple precedes the beginning of the Pharisees' prayer. "Oh Lord, thank You for making us better than other men." The old man stops eating his apple, and we see boys and men arrested in mid-action; straining not to drop a heavy sack half-unloaded from a donkey. When the prayer has finished, the old man once more begins to eat his apple; his face conveying a slight but recognisable trace of perception of this ridiculous situation.

Griffith turns in the final plea for peace to symbolic images of war and peace. They follow a pattern already set by *The Birth of a Nation,* which also ends with images heavy in symbolism. But throughout *Intolerance* Griffith introduces the symbol when the explicit will not do, or when the symbol can speak more graphically than the explicit. A scene with the mountain girl carries with it a suggestive quality rare in Griffith's work, but it is a suggestion very difficult to ignore or make excuses for. In the middle of milking a goat during the festivities of Babylon, she goes off into an ecstatic daydream, clutching the goat's teat while she sighs at the thought—surely—of "her prince" Belshazzar. Also in the Babylonian Story there is an important symbolic role played by doves, traditionally the messengers of peace. In this story, their ultimate purpose is an ironic one. Griffith introduces these several times during the festivities that follow Cyrus's retreat from the city. Belshazzar's huge bodyguard, whom we had seen previously decapitating Persians in the battle, is shown stroking a dove tenderly, while the Princess Beloved uses two doves harnessed to a miniature chariot to carry a message of love to her prince Belshazzar who sits opposite her. And it is these two doves that we see at the end of the story, already described in some detail, beside the dead Mountain Girl. The Judean Story begins at Cana in Galilee; and Griffith again uses doves here, inserting a Biblical quotation, "Be ye as harmless as doves."

Symbolism is used blatantly and without restraint as the film comes to an end, but elsewhere in the picture it furnishes some of the most touching and poignant scenes Griffith has directed. In the Modern Story, soon after the Dear One and her father have moved into their slum house, there is a small scene in which Griffith demonstrates his ability to convey in a few carefully selected details the essence of a situation. The scene is called, in a sub-title, "The Hopeful Geranium." It is a poor, half-dead plant which the Dear One keeps, but there is a small new shoot beginning to grow from the old stem. She first mourns the death of the old plant, but then visualises—in another wonderfully evocative and articulate piece of acting by Mae Marsh—the future progress of the new stem. This underlines her own predicament. Thrown out of town by the events following the strike, she and her ailing father are forced to begin a new life, while they cannot help but have a struggle to overcome the chagrin of losing their old way of life. Will their new life, as she visualises the new plant, become the embodiment of their hopes and dreams?

Finally, the whole film itself is held together by a symbol. A symbol opens the picture and likewise closes it. It is seen constantly throughout. The cradle of Humanity, eternally rocking, "ever bringing the same joys and sorrows."

Throughout this study I have repeatedly and deliberately quoted sub-titles wherever possible. D. W. Griffith above everyone else during this and later periods of the silent motion picture era has been severely criticised for his use of stylised prose in titles. Edward Wagenknecht, writing of the beautiful *Broken Blossoms,* finds his own justification for saying that "In Thomas Burke (who wrote the story), Griffith discovered, perhaps for the first time, a writer whose prose was almost as purple as his own."[8] He goes on to assert that the sub-titles are not really necessary and "can be ignored."[8] But in fact Griffith sub-titles are an integral part of his films inasmuch as they contribute to that style and overall impression that are so essentially David Wark Griffith. Already mentioned are criticisms of the nature in which Griffith introduced variants of the word "Intolerance" into his titles. But another very interesting aspect of the titles in this film arises. Miss Anita Loos, famous for her book, play and film of *Gentlemen Prefer Blondes,* claims authorship of the titles in *Intolerance.* She points out that her paraphrase of Voltaire, "When women cease to attract men, they often turn to reform as a second choice," particularly pleased Griffith in its humour, and not surprisingly, for Griffith would almost certainly have accepted a title with literary connections.[9] Therefore it is no surprise to find, also, a verse from Oscar Wilde's *Ballad of Reading Gaol* in the film, nor allusions to Herodotus, and naturally extensive quotations from the Bible. Nine years later, in an interview, Griffith again quoted Voltaire: "Voltaire said that there was nothing in fiction so dramatic, so impossible, so horrible, so banal—or so unbelievable that it couldn't be surpassed by life itself."[10] This is a concept which, for good or bad, Griffith adhered to in all of his films, and it is precisely this that many critics would like to be able to "ignore." But to ignore this, or any component of Griffith's art, is to ignore the essence of his work in the cinema.

Intolerance presents living proof of Griffith's genius as a film-maker. It is incredible that such a production could be the work of one man, as indeed to all intents and purposes it was, but this fact can only point to the conclusion that it is a genuine and sincere work. It is equally incredible that there was no script, and that Griffith edited his four stories into one continuous philosophical argument, made by touching humanities, by forceful and harrowing scenes of mass murder, and always by his ability to return again to the simplest of statements, pure and approachable by adults and children alike, for the preservation of peace and tolerance. "Not only beauty but thought is our goal," said Griffith in 1917, "for the silent drama is peculiarly the birthplace of ideas."[11]

4. Thomas Harper Ince

IF D. W. GRIFFITH was the most important and perceptive director of the era, Thomas Ince was its most important creative producer. Each man in his own way contributed much towards the furtherance of the cinema as an art. Each man has had his share of praise and criticism.

In 1920 Louis Delluc wrote of Ince: "Griffith, c'est l'homme d'hier. Ince est celui d'aujourd'hui . . . Que la renommée de Griffith l'emporte sur celle d'Ince, rien de plus juste et cela n'a pas grande importance. Griffith est le premier réalisateur cinématographique. Ince est le premier prophète."[28] In a critical study of Ince's films some thirty-six years later, George C. Pratt was to comment: "There has been haphazard survival of some of the Ince two-reelers, and of some of the later feature films. The best of these indicate that the reputation of Thomas H. Ince has suffered unmerited decline. They support the assertion of Julian Johnson (in an issue of *Photoplay* in 1917) that Ince at his height exhibited 'that peculiarly individual force, that rugged human power' that make his niche 'a distinctly individual one that no one else can fill.' "[29]

Unfortunately, in recent years, left-wing film critics have praised Ince's work only out of a desire to denigrate D. W. Griffith and what they believe to have been his "Fascist" outlook. It has been difficult to discover the true worth and the true story of Ince and his films.

THOMAS HARPER INCE was born in Newport, Rhode Island on November 16, 1882. There were two other sons in the family, John and Ralph. (The last became a fairly important film director in his own right, but like Ince he died while still a comparatively young man, as a result of a motor car accident in London in 1937.) Ince, following the family profession, became an actor; one of the most notable plays in which he is said to have appeared was James A. Herne's production of *Shore Acres*. He appeared on Broadway in *Hearts Courageous,* and according to Terry Ramsaye first met and became friendly with William S. Hart.[37] At about the same time he met and married a young actress named Alice Kershaw.

In the summer of 1910, Ince was out of work, and decided to accept an offer to appear in a film for Carl Laemmle's Imp Company. At the

same time, Mrs. Ince was appearing in American Biograph productions, and she persuaded her director, Frank Powell, to find a small part for her husband in a comedy that he was directing—*His New Lid,* a half-reeler about a new hat.

Ince made only the one film at Biograph, before returning to Imp in December 1910 to become a director. His first film was titled *Little Nell's Tobacco,* and featured Hayward Mack. In an interview with Harry Carr, published shortly after Ince's death, Carl Laemmle gives a highly romanticised picture of why he engaged Ince:

"Along came this young fellow, Ince. We gave him a job as an extra first at $5 a day, but finally we were paying him $60 a week.

"I made up my mind to give him a job as a director, and I'll tell you just why I did it. I noticed, in the first place, that he was strong and healthy physically, so he could stand the hard work. I saw that he had enthusiasm, and, although he had nice pleasant manners, he had guts and decision. Also he was a good actor."

Mary Pickford, Biograph's most promising newcomer, was lured over to Imp by Carl Laemmle, and in January 1911 Ince was assigned to direct all of her pictures. The first production featuring Mary and directed by Ince was *Their First Misunderstanding.* So infuriated were the heads of American Biograph by the "capture" of one of their stars, and by Laemmle's saucy advertising, "Little Mary is an Imp now," that with the backing of the Patents Company, they planned legal action. Pickford, Ince and Laemmle's general manager, C. A. "Doc" Willat were forced to flee America, and to continue making pictures in Cuba. Ince was on his own now; he had no one to whom he could turn for advice; he had to learn all he could of the techniques of film directing by the simple process of trial or error.

In the autumn of 1911 Mary Pickford left Imp for Reliance Majestic, and shortly afterwards Ince also parted company with Carl Laemmle. He was hired by Kessel and Bauman's New York Motion Picture Company, along with Ethel Grandin, Ray Smallwood and Charles Weston. Ince's first production for his new company was *The New Cook,* starring Ethel Grandin, and filmed at Kessel and Bauman's Edendale Studios in Los Angeles (later to become the Mack Sennett Studios). Ince has

Thomas Harper Ince

*Ince, W. S. Hart
and real Sioux Indians*

written: "My first picture contained fifty-three scenes, and it was freely predicted that I would be fired for wasting so much time and film. Around the studio I was generally designated as 'one of those New York guys that know all about the picture business.' My salutatory was a comedy. I believe it was three days in the making."[25]

Ince took an active dislike to the type of Westerns that he was supposed to direct. "They ride uphill on Thursday and downhill on Tuesday," he complained. He persuaded Kessel and Bauman to hire the Miller Bros. 101 Ranch Circus at a fee of $2,000 a week. The Circus supplied him with all the extras that he needed to produce "real" West-

erns; there were three hundred horses, buffaloes, covered wagons, tee-
pees, cowboys and about fifty real Indians. No longer would Mexicans
need to be disguised as Indians, or George Gebhardt try to convince an
audience that he was an Indian chief. The first film produced featuring
the Circus was *War on the Plains,* released on February 23, 1912; Ethel
Grandin was the heroine and Ray Myers was the boy. It was the first
two-reeler to be released by the New York Motion Picture Company.
The Company produced no more one-reelers; in 1912 they released
twenty-seven two-reelers and three three-reelers.

Around this time Ince acquired some 20,000 acres of land, known as the Santa Ynez Canyon. Here Ince built his studios, which were to come to be known as Inceville. W. E. Wing wrote of a visit to Inceville in a 1913 issue of *The New York Dramatic Mirror*:

"He began with one little stage. Since that time he has extended construction throughout the mountains, each colony laid in its suitable and logical location. With more than seven hundred people on hand and an investment of $35,000 in buildings, Ince now is the proud manager of an organization as complete as a municipality. His shops construct everything from uniforms and furniture to houses. His cultivated lands feed the multitude. His range of locations travels in leaps and bounds from naval battles on the broad Pacific to the wild West, mountain life, Ireland and the Orient and in fact to every country save the extremely tropical."

In the early days of Inceville, Ince would film all day, returning to edit the day's film in his Los Angeles bungalow. "The kitchen was outfitted to serve as a projection room where he and his wife would cut and assemble scenes made a day previous, using a meat chopper clamp to hold the reel on the table or sink. She reeled out the film while he looked at it, and it ended up in a clothes basket on the floor."[29]

Ince's first three-reeler, *Custer's Last Fight,* was completed in June 1912, and released in October of the same year. It featured Francis Ford (brother of John) as Custer, and was described by the *New York Dramatic Mirror* as "a marvellous achievement of the art."

Until the summer of 1912 Ince directed all the productions himself, with Ray C. Smallwood as his cameraman. Then in June of that year, he divided the Company between himself and Francis Ford. Ford was supplied with a detailed shooting script, written by Ince with either Richard V. Spencer (his first scenario writer) or William H. Clifford, and Ford was expected to shoot his pictures precisely according to the script. Here we have the fundamental difference between Ince and Griffith. While Ince was always to insist upon the use of a detailed scenario, if Griffith was given a script, the first thing that he would do would be to tear it up.

On June 1, 1913, Ince released his biggest production to date, *The Battle of Gettysburg,* five reels in length. Eight cameras were used simultaneously to shoot the battle scenes, and the reviewer in the *New York Dramatic Mirror* commented, "No amount of printed description could bring home, as does this picture, the magnitude of the Battle of Gettysburg and the terrible slaughter it brought. It is a wonderful visualization of the greatest battle in American history."

By the end of 1913 Ince had ceased to direct any of his productions himself, but he still edited each production, and supervised the writing of the detailed shooting script. In an interview in 1918, Ince gave his views on film directing: "The artist who essays to direct must possess an intangible something over and above the knowledge of the technique of his art. The most important asset is an intuitive and appreciative understanding of human nature in all its manifestations. The director, in the speaking drama, must know intimately the value and limitations of the material at his disposal. To get the best results he must know his people, not only as artistes, but as human beings. He must know how to humour them, how to coax and cajole them into using his ideas, when they are convinced that their own ideas are infinitely superior. The same thing holds true in the motion picture world—with added difficulties, as the work is in a way more complicated, and the effects have to be produced more rapidly."[24]

WILLIAM S. HART was put under contract by Ince in 1914. Hart was already an established stage actor; he had played the title roles in *Ben-Hur* and *The Virginian,* as well as appearing opposite Madame Modjeska in *Camille.* He was in his films, as *Variety* commented at the time of his death, "the epitome of what millions of boys of a past generation imagined they themselves would like to have been when they reached manhood. He represented to them the supreme symbol of law and order."

Hart's first film for Ince, a two-reeler titled *The Bargain,* was released in November 1914. It was one of the first Westerns to be specially written for the screen (by Ince and William H. Clifford), and in it Hart played Jim Stokes, a bandit who is taught the error of his ways by the heroine, played here by Clara Williams. It was a role that Hart was to essay time and time again in his films; the bad guy who finds out in time that he has been "riding the wrong trail."

Typical of Hart's early films, produced by Ince and directed by Reginald Barker, is *Hell's Hinges.* Hart is an outlaw in a small town, to which a young, inexperienced minister and his sister are sent. The minister is seduced by the town vamp, Louise Glaum, and his church is

Above, William S. Hart on location with director Lambert Hillyer Right, Hell's Hinges: *the new minister is seduced by the town vamp (Louise Glaum) (above); Hart stands by and watches the saloon keeper encourage the drunken mob to burn down the church (below)*

burnt down by a drunken mob. Hart stands by watching all this happen, but he is impressed by the sincerity of the minister's sister, and realises the error of his ways. Together, they and the "good" inhabitants of the town set out to build a new community. The final scenes of the destruction by fire of *Hell's Hinges,* with the flaming cross above the church, are most impressive, and the script of C. Gardiner Sullivan contrasts well the degeneration of the minister with the gradual reformation of Hart.

Hart and Ince did not work well together, and soon quarreled. Hart would not allow Ince to supervise his films, and in his autobiography, Hart describes Ince as "ruthless, conniving and selfish."

Sessue Hayakawa made his screen *début* with Ince in the 1914 six-reel production of *The Wrath of the Gods.* Hayakawa had only a small part in the picture; the leading lady was his wife Tsura Aoki. She played Toya San opposite Frank Borzage as Tom Wilson. The film was directed by Reginald Barker, and the special effects (including a volcanic eruption) of Raymond B. West were noteworthy. Discussing a later

Sessue Hayakawa

"Japanese" production of Ince, George C. Pratt has commented that "the face of Sessue Hayakawa recalls the actor prints of the Japanese artist Sharaka."[29]

By 1916 the Inceville Studios comprised five stages, the biggest one being three hundred feet by one hundred feet, and the other four seventy-five feet by fifty feet. Working under the personal supervision of Ince were eight directors: Raymond B. West, Charles Swickard, Reginald Barker, Walter Edwards, Charles Giblyn, Charles Miller, Scott Sydney and W. S. Hart. The leading players were Bessie Barriscale, Howard Hickman, Rhea Mitchell, Clara Williams, Louise Glaum, Enid Markey, J. Barney Sherry and Herschel Mayall. The head of the scenario department was C. Gardner Sullivan, and his assistants included Richard V. Spencer, J. G. Hawks, Monte M. Katterjohn, Frank Tannehill, Larier Bartlett, James Montgomery and D. F. Whitcomb. Robert Brunton was the art director and production manager, and the cameramen included Joseph H. August and Clyde de Vinna.

Many stage stars came to Inceville to make their screen *débuts,* among whom were H. B. Warner, Franklin Ritchie, Frank Keenan, Lew Cody, Lewis Stone, Mary Boland, Gladys Brockwell and Billie Burke. The last was paid $40,000 for five weeks work in the film *Peggy,* a salary which was said to have been the highest ever paid at that time to an actress for one film. Ince had fond memories of *Peggy*; he wrote: *"Peggy* was one of the greatest photoplays ever made to my manner of thinking, both as to star, the cast, which included William H. Thompson, William Desmond, Charles Ray and others, and the photography. All of the beautiful light effects were obtained without the use of an artificial light. (As a matter of fact I never used imitation sunlight until we moved to Culver City.) The direct rays of the sun and the use of mirrors were the only mediums used in the filming of *Peggy.*"[25]

Another of the players in *Peggy,* Charles Ray, was known as the "Ince Wonder Boy." **CHARLES EDGAR RAY** was born in Jacksonville, Illinois, in 1891, and from his early youth had always wanted to be an actor. In December 1912 he heard that the Ince Studios were hiring young actors, and so Ray presented himself at the Studio, and was hired by Charles Giblyn. His parts became more and more important, but after a while he became almost typecast as the shy, country boy. In his most famous Ince film, *The Coward,* released in October 1915, Ray

Charles Ray with Frank Keenan in The Coward

Charles Ray in characteristic role

plays a young Confederate soldier, who is so frightened by the battle that he deserts, but he later vindicates himself by an act of heroism. DeWitt Bodeen, who has seen the film in recent years, wrote, "compared to his performance, those of veteran players, Frank Keenan and Gertrude Claire are ham."[35]

Ray was loyal to Ince for many years, but by 1920 he had tired of the roles that Ince demanded he play, and he left to form his own company. In an interview with *Picturegoer* in 1926 Ray said: "Any man who claims to be an actor should be able to play all parts, and I could never be happy merely as a 'type.' I have always had a definite goal, and that goal has been artistic, uplifting, psychological drama."[36] He sunk all his money into *The Courtship of Myles Standish,* released in

1923. The film was a financial disaster, and Ray could not find employment. Only Ince showed him kindness, and gave him leading roles in two of his (Ince's) last productions, *Dynamite Smith* and *Percy*. The death of Ince meant the end for Ray; no good film roles came his way. His film parts got smaller and smaller, but Ray never forgot his principles. "I would much rather play the sort of roles that I like, and that I feel are fundamentally true, and remain a poor man all my life, than make a compromise and have millions in the bank."[36] He died penniless and forgotten on November 23, 1943.

To understand what happened next in Ince's career, it is necessary to look back to 1912. In this year Mutual was founded by Henry E. Aitken and John R. Freuler. Mutual released the product of American Flying A, Majestic, Thanhouser, Reliance, and the New York Motion Picture Company. The last had been founded by Kessel and Bauman in 1909, and its releases were known under the brand name of Kay Bee (the initials of its owners). In 1912, Keystone was born, and became part of the New York Motion Picture Company. The following year Griffith left Biograph and joined the now amalgamated Reliance-Majestic.

Early in 1915, Aitken resigned from Mutual, taking with him the output of the New York Motion Picture Company and Reliance-Majestic. Aitken's associated companies, Ince's Kay Bee, Sennett's Keystone and Griffith's Reliance-Majestic became the new Triangle Film Corporation, formed in the summer of 1915. Their slogan was "Triangle is the sign that says—Come in." Aitken announced that "Triangle would take the greatest stars of the stage in their greatest plays and translate them to the screen in productions that would establish new standards."

The first programme of Triangle productions opened at New York's Knickerbocker Theatre on September 23, 1915. The films included were Mack Sennett's *My Valet* with Raymond Hitchcock; *The Lamb* with Douglas Fairbanks, directed by Christy Cabanne and supervised by D. W. Griffith; and *The Iron Strain* with Dustin Farnum, Louise Glaum and Enid Markey, directed by Reginald Barker and supervised by Thomas Ince.

1916 saw the production of the most famous of all Thomas Ince films, *Civilization*. The film opens with a prologue exhorting one's love for one's neighbour and the blessings of peace. (The prologue, together

Count Ferdinand (Howard Hickman)
confronts the emperor in Civilization

with the epilogue, was the idea of Irvin Willat, who was one of the cameramen on the production. One critic described the prologue as "somewhat unduly prolonged.")

The story opens with shots of a happy and contented country, with corn ripening in the fields and children playing, "turning to mirth all things of earth as only children can." In the imperial palace, the Emperor of Woedpoyd (or Wredpyd—different prints use different spellings) signs a declaration of war, with the backing of his cabinet, with the exception of Luther Rolf, a Socialist (J. Frank Burke).

In the following scenes, the audience is introduced to Count Ferdinand (Howard Hickman), who has invented a submarine, and his *fiancée,* Katherine (Enid Markey), who is a member of a women's Peace Society. Katherine enrolls Ferdinand as a half-hearted member of the Society.

The war begins, and the scenes of battle and the destruction of townships, the young men being forced to fight, are contrasted with the earlier scenes of the contented country. Count Ferdinand is placed in command of a submarine, and while at sea he is ordered to sink the liner Propatria (some sources call the liner Arcadia). Just as the crew are loading the torpedoes, Ferdinand remembers the pleas of Katherine for peace, and has a vision of the innocent passenger's impending fate. He throws open his coat, revealing the emblem of the Peace Society pinned on his chest. He draws a gun, holds the crew at bay, and opens a sluice flooding the submarine, which eventually blows up.

The body of the Count is rescued by a boat crew from a destroyer. There then follows a long sequence in which Ferdinand in a dream enters an underground cavern, representing purgatory. Christ (George

The final scene in Civilization

Fisher) appears to him, and informs Ferdinand that his body will live again, animated by the spirit of Christ, to spread the gospel of Peace. Count Ferdinand miraculously recovers, and returns to his country.

He preaches peace outside the palace, but he is jeered at and mocked by the populace. The Emperor orders his arrest, and as the soldiers bring him before the Emperor at which point is cut in a shot showing Christ overcome by the burden of His cross. Ferdinand is court martialed, and sentenced to death.

Meanwhile, the Peace movement is growing, and the women of the nation arise and march on the palace, each wearing what would appear to be the habit of a nun. They kneel in the rain in front of the palace and pray for peace. The Emperor is told of Ferdinand's death, and goes to his cell. He sees the spirit of Christ, which takes him through a hole in the wall of the cell and shows him the horror of the war for which he is responsible. The Emperor is shown the Book of Judgement, with his name on a blood stained page.

The Emperor tells the cabinet that he will sign a peace treaty with the enemy. The final scenes show the gradual return to peace and normality in the countryside. There is a moving scene of Kate Bruce (the mother of many early Griffith-directed Biographs) welcoming her son home from the war. The prologue, very reminiscent of *Intolerance,* pictures a shepherd tending his sheep and nursing a white dove. The dove leaves the shepherd's hands, and lands on the ruins of a broken cannon.

In a foreword to the film, Ince wrote: "This is an allegorical story about war—it does not concern itself about which side is right or wrong, but deals with those ranks which are paying the grim penalty—the ranks of humanity." According to George Mitchell, President Wilson appeared with Ince in a foreword to the film photographed at Wilson's summer home, "Shadow Lawn," by Lambert Hillyer.[27]

The film has the highest ideals, and to Ince must go the credit for having the courage to present such a film at this time. But the story is far from satisfactory; the characters are dull, and one never feels that one gets to know them, and the direction by Raymond B. West is equally dull and lifeless.

The film received mixed criticism when it first appeared. *The Motion Picture Magazine* wrote: *"Civilization* is more than the magnum opus of a great director, a skilled producer, a powerful preacher—it is the passionate feeling, human breath of a master poet. Handicapped with a mediocre cast and a partisan text, Ince has so handled his effects and story, his characters and their emotions that the living, breathing whole is a photoplay of convincing beauty. In many respects it is the finest thing that has yet been done, rivalling, if not surpassing, *The Birth of a Nation, Cabiria* and all the other super features." The English trade paper, *The Bioscope,* was not so enthusiastic: "It is altogether possible that the spectacular scenes of the play would ensure its commercial success if they were not mixed up with what is described as an 'allegory.' We cannot think that it is the time to advocate any measures which might tend to relax the determination of the British public to prosecute the war to its final conclusion."

In fact, an English version of the film in a vastly modified form was released under the title of *What Every True Britain Is Fighting For.* This version showed recruiting scenes in Whitehall, and a young recruit idolising a portrait of Lord Kitchener.

Civilization was first shown in New York at the Criterion, in competition to *The Fall of a Nation,* being screened at the Liberty Theatre. *The Fall of a Nation* was written by the Rev. Thomas Dixon and Bartley Cushing, and was intensely anti-German. The film showed the invasion and subjugation of America by German soldiers, until eventually after many humiliations the country rises and drives the invaders out. The film contained cruel caricatures of William J. Bryan and Henry Ford, and in one scene an officer of the Kaiser rubs the words, "Equality, Liberty and Fraternity" from a blackboard, and substitutes the words, "Authority, Obedience and Efficiency."

The two stars of *Civilization* both had strange later careers. Enid Markey became Jane to the first screen Tarzan, Elmo Lincoln. Howard Hickman became a director, and was responsible for the charming 1920 Mae Marsh vehicle, *Nobody's Kid.* From the Thirties onwards until the time of his death he was a character actor, turning up in dozens of Hollywood films. He is perhaps best remembered for his portrayal of John Wilkes in *Gone with the Wind.*

The music for *Civilization* was composed by Victor Schertzinger. As Mrs. Ince points out (in a letter to Anthony Slide), "Mr. Ince chose the music for each picture and sent out the music with each film. Then he met Victor, who was conducting the orchestra in the old Morosco

THOMAS H. INCE STUDIOS
Culver City, California

The new Ince studios at Culver City

Theater here, and Victor took on the choosing and later wrote, that is composed, the music for specials like *Civilization*. I think the first picture he composed for was *Peggy*." The music for *The Fall of a Nation* was the work of Victor Herbert. Apart from heading Ince's music department, Schertzinger became a director in his own right; two of his best pictures are *One Night of Love* (1934) and *The Road to Singapore* (1940).

Other popular productions from Ince at this time included *The Beggar of Cawnpore,* directed by Charles Swickard with H. B. Warner; *Wolf Woman,* directed by Walter Edwards with Louise Glaum; and *The Clodhopper,* directed by Victor Schertzinger with Charles Ray.

In 1918 Ince quarrelled with Aitken, and left Triangle. He built new studios at Culver City, and signed a distribution contract with Para-

Human Wreckage: *Mrs. Wallace Reid and Bessie Love*

mount-Artcraft. These Culver City Studios were later used as a trade mark by David O. Selznick productions, and are now used by Desilu Productions. Films produced here included *Vive la France*, directed by Roy William Neill and starring Dorothy Dalton (a new Ince discovery) and *Behind the Door,* directed by Irvin Willat with Hobart Bosworth and Wallace Beery.

The following year, Ince took his productions to Metro, and formed Associated Producers Inc. with Mack Sennett, Marshall Neilan, Allan Dwan, George Loane Tucker, Maurice Tourneur and J. Parker Read.

The last two important films of Thomas Ince were both produced in 1923; they were *Human Wreckage* and *Anna Christie*. The former was scripted by C. Gardner Sullivan and photographed by Henry Sharp. The film featured Mrs. Wallace Reid (Dorothy Davenport), and used surrealist effects to depict the vision of an addict under the influence

Anna Christie: *Eugenie Besserer and George Marion*

of drugs. (Wallace Reid had died as a result of drug addiction.) Both *Human Wreckage* and *Anna Christie* were directed by John Griffith Wray, who was probably the most important director working for Ince in the Twenties.

Of *Anna Christie* Ince is supposed to have said, "I made that one for the highbrow critics who say Tom Ince can't make anything but box-office pictures." It was the first time that Eugene O'Neill had been brought to the screen.

The film was a critical success. *The New York Times* critic wrote: "Here is a picture with wonderful characterization that tells a moving and compelling story—a film that is intensely dramatic, and one that will win new audiences for the screen." Of Blanche Sweet, who played the title role, *The New York Times* said, "Miss Sweet seems to do some marvellous acting through this story, and she seems to glow with the

A perfect characterisation of Anna Christie *by Blanche Sweet*

idea of a newly discovered life in her love for Burke. It would be difficult to imagine any actress doing better in this exacting role."

In 1924 Thomas Ince went to spend a weekend on William Randolph Hearst's yacht; Ince wished to film certain stories that had appeared in Hearst's *Cosmopolitan Magazine*. He became ill on board the yacht, and returned home to Los Angeles, where he died on November 19, 1924 as a result of what would now be called a thrombosis. (Much scandal has been written about the death of Thomas Ince, and readers would be well advised to see the letter from Mrs. Ince to George Pratt printed in the Spring 1970 issue of *The Silent Picture*.)

Frederick J. Ellis wrote of him: "Thomas H. Ince to the audience of the world, 'T. H.' to his studio employees, Tom to his friends, and Tommie to the more intimate of those friends, was one of the little group of pioneers that have blazed the trail for the generations of directors and producers that will follow. One of the sad aspects of the lives of movie makers is that their work is as pictures traced on the sand, to be effaced by the tides of time. The painter leaves his canvases, the author his books, the sculptor his statues, the architect his cathedrals, and the musician his operas or ballads. The producer and director leave negatives and prints, but these are destroyed or consigned to the oblivion of the storage vault. The Ince productions that are completed or in production will be exhibited for a few months. Some may be re-shown a few times, in memory of their maker—and that will be the end. But Tom Ince will be a name held in glorious memory so long as there remains a living being who has witnessed one of his pictures. Ince, Griffith and the others had no precedent to follow. They had to form their own technique. They are to their successors, what the dramatists of Greece were to the playwrights of today."[23]

5. The Denial of Spectacle: True Heart Susie to Broken Blossoms

WITHIN THE SPACE of two years Griffith had suddenly found himself at the head of his profession. What was he to produce next? *Intolerance* was already an undisputed artistic success and in it many directors had found ample material on which to build their own particular styles and also seen in it ideas which they were able to expand themselves; ideas not only in the intellectual sense but also technical ideas. And so, following the appearance of this gargantuan picture, all eyes were on Griffith: what was he to produce that could top *Intolerance?* *The Birth of a Nation* itself had seemed at the time the peak of his achievement. But Griffith had improved upon it. *Intolerance* now seemed the ultimate; it stood firmly ahead of any films which sought to improve on *The Birth of a Nation.* Once seen, Griffith's two epic productions would form the basis for all film production. Others would imitate them, take the ideas found within them, and build upon them, or, which is nonetheless valid, react violently against them and all they stood for and Griffith himself.

For the film student of today, looking at Griffith's prodigious output chronologically, the films made following *Intolerance* must come as a welcome pause for breath. There is so much concentrated creative talent in Griffith's films up to 1917 that each film—including the later Biograph pictures—demands detailed study in order that it may be fully appreciated.

To the audiences of 1917 however, indeed to the industry itself, it seemed as if Griffith had reached the peak and was now on the downward path when the next film he produced was neither longer nor on a grander scale than *Intolerance.* It was assumed then, as it is even now, that an artistic success, if duplicated faithfully, will be just as much a success the second time around. Griffith knew better.

During a visit to Britain with *Intolerance,* Griffith was asked, and accepted, to make a film for the Allies. After filming both in Britain and on the Western Front, Griffith eventually released *Hearts of the World,* but the Armistice was signed before the film's completion and

Hearts of the World: *a prewar idyll.*
Dorothy Gish and (right) Noel Coward

he had radically to re-think his original concept in the light of the new peace. The film is an excellent example of Griffith's singular talent for portraying human suffering by focussing on one or two carefully characterised individuals whose personal tragedies reflect the greater events in which they are inevitably involved. Indeed, any attempt by Griffith at straightforward documentary was clearly not considered; he said at the time, "Viewed as a drama, the war is disappointing."[15]

Hearts of the World: *Lillian Gish finds Robert Harron on the battlefield*

Here, in *Hearts of the World,* we again find the common theme of Griffith's more successful pictures; woman's maturity. Lillian Gish as the Girl matures from the girlish innocence of praying that the Boy will always love her at the beginning of the film, surrounded by farm animals, to the woman at the climax of the picture, when she is able to kill one of the advancing German officers when the action is called for. She begins by playing with ducks, and by the end of the picture she is a fully aware mature woman, knowledgeable of life's miseries and suffering, and, finally and possibly most important for Griffith, its happinesses.

Although Griffith showed many times that he could handle with complete dexterity a subject of epic proportions, indeed that he could produce a work of great complexity and moreover do so in a single-handed fashion keeping the essence of the subject in his head, nevertheless there is a great deal to be learned about the man and his ideals and ideas in his less ambitious work. It may be added that these smaller films often achieve the emotional intensity found in his more expansive films.

After completing *Hearts of the World,* Griffith made several films still taking as their theme the First World War, incorporating footage shot in France for the first picture, while at the same time starting production on *Broken Blossoms,* which was to be his next major work after *Hearts of the World.* Of the five films between these two pictures, only two had themes which were not connected to war. One, *A Romance of Happy Valley,* and a second, similar in theme, *True Heart Susie.*

Although on the surface this modest little film might possibly appear slight, it must surely give insight to the mind and objectives of D. W. Griffith. The story involves a childhood romance between Susie (Lillian Gish) and William (Robert Harron). Unknown to William, who believes he owes his further education to an unknown benefactor, Susie herself sacrifices much in order to pay for his ministerial training. He is still ignorant of Susie's sacrifices on his graduation however, and marries Bettina, a woman of dubious character who is simply after William's money. But, as the title suggests, Susie never falters in her secret love for William, although all her romantic dreams seem to disintegrate. Before too long Bettina drifts back to the fast-living set she had left for a more sombre life with William, and becomes disillusioned with marriage. One night she slips away to a party and soon finds she is in the company that suits her best. She returns in a storm and discovers that she has mislaid her key, and so is obliged to seek hospitality with Susie, first making sure that Susie will shield her before William. Susie is naturally reluctant to lie to William on any account, much less protect a woman she knows to be false and without virtue, but eventually agrees when her compassion gets the better of her. As a result of her exposure during the storm, Bettina becomes seriously ill and dies before she can confess to William the reason for her end. Through Susie's mother, William learns the truth about who paid for his training, but still refuses to betray the memory of his wife, who he still believes to have been faithful. At length he learns the truth about this

too, and is freed at last from his oath and proposes to Susie. Their marriage brings her dreams to a sweet reality.

Many commentators have noted the great charm of this picture, as well as moments of deep emotional intensity. An outstanding performance from Lillian Gish elevates the character from the near-ridiculous to moments of the sublime, especially in the scenes in which she is torn between love and duty. Her gentle caressing of Bettina after giving her shelter from the storm has a simplicity and sincerity which could so easily have slipped into the farcical. When she discovers William in the arms of Bettina after assuring herself that having seen Bettina in the arms of another man minutes before meant that William intended to ask for her own hand, the restrained grief on her face and the tears that well up in her eyes during one long and continuous close-up convey the very essence of a rejected devotion. And through the tears a forced smile, the recognition of what she imagines as her presumption to William's love, produces a scene which even Miss Gish herself has rarely equalled. That smile, that shot, would alone justify the whole of Griffith's work, for it embodies all that is Griffith and all that is Gish and the two talents combine to produce a perfect *cinematic* whole. It is one of those extraordinary moments in the cinema.

Apart from many moments of tenderness and one or two scenes of charming coyness, there is a sequence of strong drama when Bettina arrives back from her party to find that she is locked out without a key. In her anguished groping for a crack in the window frame as the rain runs down the walls in torrents resembling the texture of oil, the photography giving it a dark, menacing quality, Bettina's panic is all too credible.

Although those of Susie and William are the dominant characters, the characterisation of Bettina is probably the most important. It is she, after all, who comes between them, and at the same time facilitates the proof of Susie's lasting and genuine love for William. A scene in which Susie sees Bettina kissing another man (this immediately before Bettina accepts William's offer of marriage) provides the key to her character and her situation. It is perhaps the key scene of the film itself.

True Heart Susie: *William (Robert Harron) marries Bettina (Clarine Seymour), while Susie (Lillian Gish) looks on wistfully*

It is night, and Bettina is on a verandah with a boy friend. They embrace, unaware that they are observed by Susie, and just at that moment a window flies open flooding them in light from William's house. As it happens no one is in the room and they escape unnoticed (so they think).

The significance of this scene is made clear when we consider Bettina's character in relation to the others. She marries for money only; it is a loveless marriage although William believes himself in love with her (while refusing to acknowledge Susie's love for him). This is an underhand action which will be brought to light at least twice when William will suspect her fidelity but when his own simple trust and blindness will prevent him from seeing her treachery. It is always Susie who recognises Bettina's inconstancy.

It is only after Bettina's death, and even then after conclusive proof of her unfaithfulness that William is able to see again, and it is only then that he is able for the first time to recognise his own true passion and Susie's true heart.

Technically, the picture has few pretensions, and it is for this reason that it is successful as a work of art. It is simple, straightforward, and utterly modest. Griffith makes much use of flashback to point characters' feelings, especially those of Susie's, whose dreams of marriage and happiness with her beloved William never lose their charming naïveté, even when they come true. Griffith ends the picture with a shot of Susie and William hand in hand as they were at the start of the picture, and a subtitle the essence of which is, "and we can suppose that the couple walk hand in hand as they did when children." In fact it is the end of the film that is weakest. Susie matures into a woman during the course of the action—a recurring Griffith theme— but when William eventually proposes she lapses uncomfortably back to her girlish coyness which dominated the beginning of the film.

In all of Griffith's pictures there is a certain amount of unashamed sentimentality; in *True Heart Susie* there is more than in most; but Lillian Gish lifts the film to moments of real poignancy and real emotional intensity, with a performance full of the happinesses and of the sadnesses of life as Griffith saw and portrayed them.

True Heart Susie was made almost concurrently with *Broken Blossoms* and in fact was released shortly after *Broken Blossoms*. It is perhaps for this reason that the former picture is not, or has not been, more highly regarded than perhaps it should have been. It is true, however, that in comparison, *Broken Blossoms* is unquestionably the greater picture. Whilst *True Heart Susie* has a certain atmosphere, it is nevertheless of a nebulous nature and *Broken Blossoms* in comparison carries with it the "rendition of London fogs, the lights and shadows, the tinted stock in soft blues, oranges and golds, the grays, the browns, the lovely soft-focus photography."[2] (Eileen Bowser) The film portrays, almost in an impressionist style, the love between an unassuming and deeply compassionate Chinaman (Richard Barthelmess) and a maltreated girl whose guardian, "Battling" Burrows, tortures her physically and mentally. Lillian Gish as Lucy the girl gave for Griffith all her expertise and soul to this part, as she had offered her gifts for every picture they had made, and were to make, together.

The wonder of this picture is the fusion of directorial and acting style.

The impressionistic style of Broken Blossoms

I have already mentioned how the film prompts us to think of the impressionist school of painting; images seem almost to blend from one to another and certain shots—of no great importance in the film as a whole—leave an indelible stamp on the memory: people walking down a misty London street, Lucy wandering along deserted wharves, seem to be dream-like figures in an imaginary landscape.

Broken Blossoms was made entirely in a studio and this undoubtedly accounts for the film's great atmospherics. The picture includes a famous scene often shown as an extract which does justice neither to the film as a whole nor to the extract nor to Griffith nor to Miss Gish. The scene is the so-called "closet" scene, where Lillian Gish locks herself in a cupboard in order to get away from the enraged Burrows, who has discovered that she and the Chinaman had spent several hours under the same roof and alone—a fact which to a bigot such as himself is intolerable. It is certainly true that this particular sequence, leading up to and including its climax within the closet, is one of the rare

Broken Blossoms: *Lillian Gish cornered*

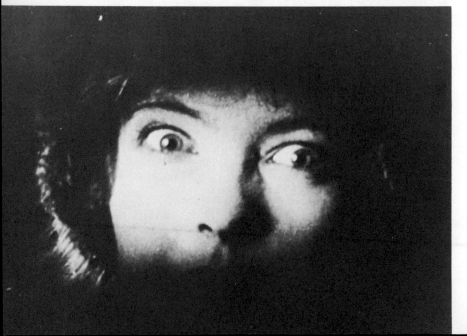

Broken Blossoms: *Cheng Huan (Richard Barthelmess) shoots Burrows*

moments in silent film history where the power of the image attains an almost aural perspective. Griffith achieves this kind of effect more than once in his work—Mae Marsh alone in her room in *Intolerance* after the trial in which her husband has been sentenced to death carries with it the same feeling.

If Lillian Gish's performance in *Broken Blossoms* is to be counted among her greatest screen roles, as I believe it should, then the performance of Richard Barthelmess is her perfect complement. His Chinese is portrayed as a deeply reverent and compassionate man whose love for peace is equalled only by his love for beauty. He finds both qualities when he shelters Lucy from the savageries of Burrows. In the end he is corrupted by the forces which surround him—those that he despises, of violence and intolerance—when he comes face to face with Burrows. Too late to save Lucy, too late to save even him-

self he throws himself into the uneven struggle with determination and courage, as the final and ultimate sacrifice to Lucy and their spiritual happiness. He carries a gun—Burrows is unarmed but tries to reach a hatchet on the floor. Cheng Huan shoots—Burrows falls dead. Later, when he realises that soon the police will arrive for him, Cheng Huan stabs himself.

Thus ends this most beautiful and gentle of all Griffith's pictures, with Cheng Huan, the Chinaman whose mission was to bring the message of Buddha to the West, a message of peace and tolerance, and who becomes inextricably entangled in Western roughness and bigotry.

Broken Blossoms was a great success in mid-1919 when it first opened in New York. This was perhaps the work that everyone had been expecting to follow *Intolerance* without knowing exactly *what* they expected. As an entirely studio-made picture it had much to teach an industry which had up to now relied heavily on location work to provide any kind of effective atmosphere.

For the remainder of 1919 Griffith involved himself in three pictures, two of which demanded location work in the Caribbean, *The Idol Dancer* and *The Love Flower*. The third picture, *The Greatest Question,* was another rural picture in the style of *True Heart Susie* and marked the last appearance in a Griffith picture by Robert Harron, who died in September of 1920 from a bullet wound. Harron had been with Griffith since the beginning, in 1908, and had created many of Griffith's most telling and dramatic characters. His death remains a mystery, but all available information points conclusively to the fact that he died as a result of an accident.

The New Year, and the new decade, saw Griffith start production on his next important picture, and this film was to become, in the words of Eileen Bowser, "second only to *The Birth of a Nation* as a money-maker."[2] This film was *Way Down East*.

Richard Barthelmess

6. Into the Twenties: Way Down East and Orphans of the Storm

I N TERMS OF CINEMA HISTORY, Griffith was the man who fired the starting-pistol. It was he who gave the medium what it required to develop and expand. There came a time when he inevitably appeared to have been "left behind," a "non-starter." It was to happen that he would be attacked again and again for his refusal to participate in the race. "Your refusal to face the world," wrote one critic, "is making you more and more a sentimentalist. You see passion in terms of cooing doves or the falling of a rose petal . . . your lack of contact with life makes you deficient in humor. In other words, your splendid unsophistication is a menace to you—and to pictures." Thus wrote James Quirk in 1924, cruelly cutting down the man who had virtually furnished him with a job (inasmuch as Griffith had given to the movies what no other individual had even come near to possessing). What Quirk failed to recognise was that Griffith was not a man to be swept along in the tide of fashion. Why should he follow others? How *could* he follow others, when in effect they were following *his* precepts?

Way Down East was Griffith's longest picture since *Intolerance,* and ran for more than three hours. In terms of construction, it relies on finely interwoven detail rather than the more instantly recognisable cross-cutting that distinguished his earlier work. In the opening sequences for example, when Anna is tricked into an illegal marriage to Sanderson, the ceremony itself is full of visual commentary, with the ring falling to the floor, cutting to Bartlett (played by Richard Barthelmess) waking suddenly from a nightmare—and this before any knowledge on anyone's part of their two fates and the way they will eventually come together.

Lillian Gish as Anna has received much deserved praise for her work in this picture, especially for her superhuman feats among the ice-floes in the climactic sequences of the picture. The manner in which she receives the news of her false marriage, in the knowledge that she is pregnant, is yet another triumph for her acting ability under Griffith. The scene in which she baptises her own child as it is dying also comes

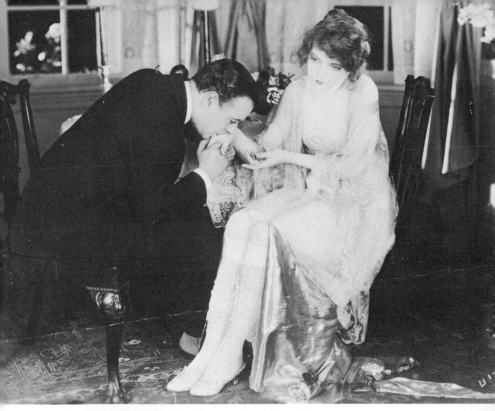

Way Down East: *the loveless marriage. Lowell
Sherman and Lillian Gish as Sanderson and Anna*

close to being one of Griffith's supreme cinematic achievements.

She also adds a sense of frightening realism to the scene in which she is told that her baby is dead. For a second or two she stares blankly into space, then slowly begins to shake her head from side to side. Suddenly, as if the news strikes her like some physical blow, she throws her head back, and, as if going into an epileptic fit, her whole body stiffens and she sits choking and screaming.

Anna eventually recovers and goes away to a town in which no one (she believes) can possibly be aware of her tragic situation, a situation which will also be regarded as shameful. She meets David Bartlett (Richard Barthelmess) and he, like many other characters in Griffith pictures, is here identified with doves in one sequence. The truth will out, however, and especially in a small town. Unknown to Anna, Sanderson is to reappear, and her secret is to become common knowledge. Bartlett is undeterred, although the rest of the town immediately brand her an evil woman. The scene in which Anna is ordered out of the house by the Squire has been excused by some who explain that it

Left, Lillian Gish. Below: Way Down East:
Squire Bartlett (Burr Mackintosh) and Anna

Way Down East: *Anna turned out into the snow. Right to left, Burr Mackintosh, Kate Bruce, Vivia Ogden, Lowell Sherman, Lillian Gish, Mary Hay, Creighton Hale, George Neville, Richard Barthelmess and Edgar Nelson*

needs dialogue for its effectiveness. On the contrary, this scene is of great emotional intensity, and this intensity is achieved simply by Griffith's editing technique. Once again, he uses visual commentary on the basic situation to replace long sequences where there should be dialogue.

Anna is sent out into the blizzard, and David runs after her. There follows some really remarkable photography, shots in which Anna's cape seems to vanish and reappear behind trees and snowdrifts, close-ups of Anna, whose eyelashes seem to have icicles on them, and this sequence leads directly to the chase on the ice-floes.

This sequence has achieved a great deal of notoriety over the years, and seems to have become the only part of *Way Down East* that is now

Way Down East: *The rescue from the ice*

remembered. It is certainly remarkable, but once again, it is all the more remarkable in context. Lillian Gish's well-known quote of "All that winter, whenever Mr. Griffith saw an ice cake, he wasn't satisfied till he had me on it," betrays what appears to be a sequence of perfect continuity, apart from some rather obvious cut-ins of Niagara Falls.

Way Down East was followed in 1921 by *Dream Street* in which Griffith turned once more to the stories of Thomas Burke, on whose work *Broken Blossoms* was based. Towards the end of 1921 he completed *Orphans of the Storm*. Here again was the large canvas. The French revolution was the background for a story of two orphan sisters, played by the Gish sisters. Edward Wagenknecht, in his book *The Movies in the Age of Innocence,* notes how this picture begins "as abruptly as a Biograph with the antecedent slaying of the father of

133

Epic extravagance: Joseph Schildkraut and Lillian Gish in Orphans of the Storm

the 'orphans,' creating a necessary condition for the story with the least possible expenditure of effort."[8] The parallel with those early pictures seems not to end here, for it appears, looking at *Orphans of the Storm* today, that once more Griffith was having to work within imposed conditions. However, as in the case of the Biographs, this does not make *Orphans of the Storm* an imperfect picture, and here again can be seen Griffith's faultless gift for re-creating a period, a gift that goes back to *Judith of Bethulia* and beyond.

The sequences that seem the most successful are those in which the poverty of the age is most obvious. Griffith's sense of social justice is here given the perfect setting of course, and as Wagenknecht observes, "like Dickens, Griffith approved of the French Revolution but deplored its excesses, and he could not resist telling us, in long subtitles, . . . that while the French Revolution rightly overthrew a bad government, we

—*and social realism: Schildkraut and Gish at the foot of the guillotine*

must exercise care not to exchange our good government for 'Bolshevism and license'."[8]

The familiar "Last Minute Rescue" towards the end of reel twelve is as exciting and as beautifully executed as we have by now come to expect from Griffith. Cutting between the guillotine and Henriette (Lillian Gish) and Danton (Monte Blue) racing on horseback with her pardon, the sequence is a perfect example of "stretched action," in which the time taken for Lillian Gish to walk three paces, for example, in the completed sequence, now intercut with other action, takes twice or maybe three times as long. This serves to build the suspense inasmuch as it creates an almost unbearable sense of impatience.

The crowd scenes have been likened to those of *The Birth of a Nation,* and in the emotional effect they create this is certainly valid. Griffith's approach to their arrangement had altered considerably during

Orphans of the Storm: *Griffith directs from the rostrum a scene for the final reel*

the six years that separated the two pictures, however. In *Orphans of the Storm* there is one sequence in which the crowd degenerates into a semi-delirious dance. A chain is formed and the whole crowd turns into a kind of weaving serpent. As well as photographing this scene in a straightforward manner, Griffith also chooses to retreat into a house, so that we see the crowd through a window in the square beyond. This gives a certain claustrophobic effect, and certainly the whole scene has more conscious *organisation* than its predecessors in 1914.

Although the critical reception to *Orphans of the Storm* was warm, the film was not the financial success for which Griffith had hoped.

He was to go on producing fine pictures, but he had lost the confidence of those who had marvelled at the spectacle and complexity of *The Birth of a Nation* and *Intolerance*. Slowly, he was being drawn into the Hollywood production system although he never ceased to create precedents in almost every film he made. Perhaps everyone expected an *Intolerance* every six months, instead of a *True Heart Susie* one year and a *Broken Blossoms* the next. It has to be admitted that in *Orphans of the Storm* Griffith seemed to be trying to align himself to the "sophisticated" style which his critics held as ideal. It didn't suit Griffith, and, in the end, it didn't suit the critics, for they could no longer see the artist they had once admired so strongly. The clarity seemed to be slipping out of Griffith's pictures. His early work seemed too crystal-clear; and now his films had taken on a duller edge.

*Revolution—*Orphans of the Storm. *In scenes such as this Griffith heightened the dramatic effect by masking in order to alter his screen shape*

Although these pictures do not lack Griffith's basic and intuitive flair for picture-making, they *do* lack the deep philosophical basis on which, during the period in which he had absolute independence, he was able to construct the masterpieces for which he has justly become famous. The later films may seem to aspire to philosophical heights, but rarely do they plumb the depths, or question the basic human rights in a fashion so direct and forceful as that employed in *Intolerance*.

That in 1924 a critic could have accused Griffith as a menace to pictures indicates the climate in which he had now to work. He had become caught up in the machinery which he had set in motion, and, although in retrospect his last films are as worthy and craftsmanlike as any he made, Griffith seemed to have nothing more to contribute to the technique of motion pictures. He was therefore thrown off course by the industry and critics alike, remembered only by the few who had worked with him and admired his work right from the summer of 1908, when his critics and those who were to benefit from his genius were so blissfully unaware that film had any possibilities at all.

Griffith's last film, his second talkie, was *The Struggle,* made in 1931. He died seventeen years later of a cerebral haemorrhage. Considering the treatment he received from those who were dependent on his innovations and foundations for their livelihood, it is to his lasting credit that he was not more bitter than he was. Griffith and his "birthplace of ideas" was worthy of more than he ever received.

The Orphans of the Storm *(Dorothy and Lillian Gish)*

7. The Star System

THE SECOND DECADE of the Twentieth century, as far as the American cinema is concerned, belonged very much, as the previous chapters have shown, to two men, D. W. Griffith and Thomas Ince. Working entirely apart, they, more than any other Americans, were responsible for the creation of the Hollywood system of film production.

Had the decade contributed nothing else, it would still be one of the most important eras in the history of American cinema. But this period also saw the development of one other factor that contributed much to the creation of an industry and to the supremacy of Hollywood films at the box-office—the star system. And that star system might equally be said to have been created by one person—Mary Pickford.

Little of importance has been written about **MARY PICKFORD**; writers have found it difficult to express in words the *joie de vivre,* the natural gaiety, the humanity that was Mary Pickford. C. A. Lejeune in her book, *Cinema,* published in 1931 said, "she sends us away from a picture house absurdly generous, ridiculously touched." When Mary Pickford appeared on the screen "every sprig of sentiment in an audience began to stir." Edward Wagenknecht has written: "Her films encourage, and submit to, little analysis. Thus while it is quite easy to be enthralled by Mary's antics in, say, *Rebecca of Sunnybrook Farm* as by Griffith's heroics in, say, *The Birth of a Nation,* is is more difficult to write about them."[8]

A reviewer in *The New York Dramatic Mirror* wrote: "To analyze the acting of Mary Pickford is about as satisfactory as trying to draw a definite conclusion from a metaphysical premise. After much circumlocution, after the use of many words and the expenditure of much grey matter one is forced to the inevitable conclusion that Mary Pickford is Mary Pickford. She has a charm, a manner, an expression that is all her own. She seems to have the happy faculty of becoming for the time being the character she is portraying. At no time does one

Mary Pickford: "The World's Sweetheart"

Mary Pickford in a typical American Biograph one-reeler,
The Old Actor, *with Charles West and W. Christy Miller*

gather the impression that Mary Pickford is acting. She is the epitome of naturalness. But why go on? The sum and substance of it all is that Mary Pickford is unique, and irrespective of the strength or weakness of any picture in which she appears, the fact that Mary Pickford appears in it makes it a good picture."

The unique Mary Pickford was born, Gladys Smith, in Toronto on April 8, 1893. She entered films with the American Biograph Company, and although the Company did not name any of its players (for fear that the publicity might make them swollen-headed, and demand more money), the public soon recognised and liked the small girl with the tomboyish manner and cheeky face. An unknown writer in a provincial

British newspaper, the *Letchworth Citizen* of June 25, 1910, typifies the attitude of the cinemagoing public to Mary Pickford at that time: "Each film-making firm has its own special favourites, and one of the most known at our own Picture Palace is she who takes the leading part in all the films of the American Biograph Company. From gay to grave, the quick flash of her eyes transports us, and many a lesson has she taught us by means of the characters she portrays."

In 1911 she left American Biograph to appear in films for Imp and Reliance (none of these films appear to have survived), but she returned again to Biograph in 1912.

Then in 1913, Mary Pickford left Biograph to return to the stage, and play the title role in David Belasco's *The Good Little Devil*. Belasco paid her a salary of two hundred dollars a week, after Mary had said to him, "My goal is to earn five hundred dollars a week by the time I am twenty."[13] Then one day before the play's Broadway opening. . . . "The first real intimation that I had that the films were making for themselves vast audiences. One Christmas Day, in Baltimore, Ernest Lawford, who was one of the cast, knocked on my dressing room door and called: 'There are hundreds of people waiting in the alley to see Little Mary, Queen of the Movies, leave the theater'!"[13] Mary Pickford had become a film star without realising it.

Meanwhile, on July 12, 1912, Adolph Zukor and Daniel Frohman exhibited for the first time in New York, *Queen Elizabeth,* starring Sarah Bernhardt under Louis Mercanton's direction. It was the first film distributed by their new company, Famous Players. The company's slogan became "Famous Players in Famous Plays." They opened a small studios in West 26th Street, and here filmed their first production, *The Prisoner of Zenda,* featuring a one-time Broadway *matinée* idol, James K. Hackett. This was followed by *Tess of the D'Urbevilles* with Minnie Maddern Fiske. After she had agreed to appear in a filmed play, other actresses were willing to follow suit. Lillie Langtry announced, "I am proud and happy to appear in a motion picture for contemporary audiences and future generations. To be enrolled in the Famous Player's Company's gallery of artists is a distinction that will survive myself. Through its power of perpetuity, I am immortal—I am a film."

The next play that Famous Players proposed to film was *The Good*

143

Little Devil. The film was a failure, but the meeting of Zukor and Pickford established one thing that as far as the public is concerned, the most important aspect of a film is its star. Mary was offered a contract worth five hundred dollars a week; she was nineteen years old. As James Card says, "She left the theatre for the cinema and it is scarcely an exaggeration to say that she took most of the Belasco audiences right along with her."[38]

(It is worth noting that Famous Players soon realised the value of an established screen player. In 1915 they put under contract Carlyle Blackwell and Blanche Sweet. The latter is one of the most underrated of screen actresses; it is highly probable that had she not left D. W. Griffith she would have been given the role of Elsie Stoneman in *The Birth of a Nation.*)

Edwin S. Porter was the director on *The Good Little Devil;* for her next picture, *In the Bishop's Carriage,* Mary had the services of another Edison trained director, J. Searle Dawley. Mary remained with Adolph Zukor for five and a half years. "I have no hesitation in calling them the happiest years of my screen life."[13] Miss Pickford's salary rose steadily as did her screen popularity. Samuel Goldwyn wrote that shortly before Mary's salary had reached a guaranteed level of ten thousand dollars a week, she said to him, discussing Chaplin's contract, "Just think of it, there he is getting all that money and here am I, after all my hard work, not making one half that much."[42] Her rivalry with Chaplin helped to raise her salary to a level that Zukor just would not pay. In 1918, she left to join First National. (By this date Zukor's Famous Players had merged with Samuel Goldwyn's Company and Jesse L. Lasky's Company, and together they had gained control of Paramount, formerly held by W. W. Hodkinson.)

In April 1919 the United Artists Corporation of Delaware was incorporated. It was formed by Mary Pickford, Douglas Fairbanks (Mary's second husband, she had been previously married to Owen Moore and was later to marry Charles "Buddy" Rogers), D. W. Griffith and Charlie Chaplin. A wit at the time commented, "The asylum is now in the hands of the maniacs." Mary Pickford's career was to last for many years still, and she was to rise to greater and greater heights, but I prefer to stop at this point, when Chaplin's and Pickford's careers merged. As Iris Barry wrote in her book, *Let's Go to the Pic-*

The Formation of United Artists:
Fairbanks, Griffith, Pickford and Chaplin

tures, "The two greatest names in the cinema are, I beg to reiterate, Mary Pickford and Charlie Chaplin . . . theirs are the greatest names in the cinema and from an historical point of view they always will be great."

From the Mary Pickford productions that this writer has been able to view, *Heart of the Hills, The Hoodlum* and *My Best Girl,* it is obvious that Mary Pickford more than lives up to the legend. Mary Pickford trying to outdo John Gilbert and his dancing skill in *The Heart of the*

Mary Pickford and Charles "Buddy" Rogers
in a charming love scene from My Best Girl

Hills or one of the final scenes in *My Best Girl,* in which she realises
that she is not good enough to marry "Buddy" Rogers and attempts,
through her tears, to prove to his father (Hobart Bosworth) that she
is just a fun-loving flapper—these are moments in the cinema that one
can never forget. How one envies Edward Wagenknecht, who can
write, "No other generation will ever have her as we had her . . . we
shall cherish her in our hearts as long as we live, along with the memories
of our own youth, and be grateful in troubled times for the joy she
brought us."[8]

Mary Pickford's closest rival was **MARGUERITE CLARK**, and
while it is at least possible to view Mary Pickford's films in private
collections or at the George Eastman House, none of Miss Clark's
productions are known positively to exist.

Miss Clark was known as "the four foot ten fairy," so petite and
dainty did she appear. One critic wrote of her, "she seems to have dis-

*Mary Pickford with Fairbanks and Chaplin
clowning on the set of* Pollyanna *(1919)*

covered the secret of perpetual youth; and with it moreover, to have combined the grace and charm which the wisdom of experience alone can bring."[39] Marguerite was born in Avondale, Cincinnati on February 22, 1887, and made her first stage appearance in 1899 as a member of the Strakosch Opera Company; she appeared in numerous musical shows and in 1908 could be seen in a touring version of *Peter Pan* (playing the title role).

It was while she was appearing in a revival of *Merely Mary Ann* in 1914 that Adolph Zukor first saw Miss Clark, and asked her to sign a contract with Famous Players. Her first film was *Wildflower,* directed by Allan Dwan, and released in October 1914. It soon became apparent that Miss Clark was going to be an expert film actress; reviewing her third film, *The Goose Girl,* directed by Fred Thompson, and released in 1915, *Moving Picture World* said, "she conquers her audience in an instant."

It also became very apparent that there was a definite rivalry between Pickford and Clark, especially as both were working for the same studio. The stars themselves showed little interest in each other; the rivalry was more apparent in the behaviour of the stars' respective relatives-cum-managers, Mary's mother and Marguerite's sister Cora. "The two doughty supporters of opposing causes used to look at each other about as pleasantly as did the Montagues and the Capulets," said Samuel Goldwyn.[42] The rivalry reached its height in 1918 when Mary Pickford won the *Motion Picture Magazine's* popularity contest with 158,199 votes, and Marguerite Clark came second with 138,852.

According to Edward Wagenknecht, Marguerite Clark's best picture was probably *Prunella,* directed in 1918 by Maurice Tourneur. From the stills available the film looks fascinating, and one cannot agree more with Wagenknecht that there is "no motion picture at present unavailable to students of the cinema which it would be more important to recover."[8] The stills also prove, as DeWitt Bodeen has written, that Marguerite Clark's "screen image was a compound of whimsicality and frail beauty."[34]

On August 15, 1918, Marguerite married Lieutenant Harry Palmerston Williams, and the story is that Williams insisted there could be no scenes in Miss Clark's films in which she kissed her leading man. According to Jesse L. Lasky in *I Blow My Own Horn,* "fans couldn't accept their idol as a frigid heroine. Without wasting any time or more dimes at the box office they got themselves other idols." However, a more rational explanation is put forward by Samuel Goldwyn: "Mary long outlasted her fair rival. Why was this? Marguerite Clark was beautiful, she was exquisitely graceful, and she brought to the screen a more finished stage technique and a more spacious background than did Miss Pickford. My answer to this question applies not only to Miss Clark, but to all the other actresses who have flashed, meteor-like, across the screen horizon. First of all, she did not have Mary Pickford's absorbing passion for work. Secondly, she did not possess the other artiste's capacity for portraying fundamental human emotion. Simple and direct and poignant. Mary goes to the heart, much as does a Foster

Marguerite Clark in The Goose Girl

melody. Herein is the real success of a popularity so phenomenally sustained."[42]

Marguerite Clark made her last film in 1921, *Scrambled Wives,* directed by Edward H. Griffith for her own production company. She lived happily in retirement until her death on September 25, 1940.

The final major leading lady who helped to create the star system, **MARY MILES MINTER,** did not work for Zukor until late 1919. Before discussing her career, therefore, it is worthwhile mentioning a few other personalities of the decade involved with the aforementioned companies.

Pauline Frederick, Elsie Ferguson and Marie Doro were popular stage stars who made an easy transition into films through Famous Players-Lasky. Fannie Ward appeared opposite Sessue Hayakawa in

Right, Mary Miles Minter

An inter-racial relationship on the screen: Fannie Ward and Sessue Hayakawa in The Cheat

Lasky's *The Cheat,* directed by Cecil B. DeMille in 1915, "which, not only in the savage branding scene, startled America and France into applause."[30] DeMille was responsible for the direction of the six films made between 1915 and 1917 by Geraldine Farrar. Miss Farrar was a star of the Metropolitan Opera Company, and she was the only opera singer to make a really successful career for herself in films.

Of her *Joan the Woman* (1917), Julian Johnson in *Photoplay* wrote, "Though it is not faultless, *Joan the Woman* is the best sun-spectacle since *The Birth of a Nation,* and in the opinion of the writer only that sweeping review of arms and hearts has excelled it." Miss Farrar left Lasky to make seven pictures for Goldwyn, before retiring from the screen. (Goldwyn had left Lasky in 1917 to go into independent pro-

Joan the Woman: *Geraldine Farrar and Wallace Reid*

duction with Edgar Selwyn. Stars he had under contract included Jane Cowl, Mabel Normand, Mae Marsh and another opera star, Mary Garden.)

Mary Miles Minter was far prettier than Mary Pickford, but she, unlike Miss Pickford, could not act. Although it must be admitted that when a star is as lovely to look at as Mary Miles Minter acting does not really matter. One of her directors, Edward Sloman, said of her, "Without doubt, she was the best-looking youngster I ever saw, and the lousiest actress."[12]

Despite her lack of acting ability, however, Mary Miles Minter was a serious threat at one time to Mary Pickford. When Mary Pickford left Adolph Zukor, he signed up Mary Miles Minter hoping to make her into as big a star as Pickford.

Mary Miles Minter was born, Juliet Reilly, in Shreveport, Louisiana, on April 1, 1902. She was a child actress for several years, from 1908 to 1911, before she made her first screen appearance in *The Nurse,* produced by the Powers Company. In the film she was billed as "Little Juliet Shelby" (her mother had assumed the name of Charlotte Shelby when she separated from her husband). Mary did not make another film until 1915, when she was featured as Mary Miles Minter (this was actually the name of her cousin, who had died at the age of eight) in *The Fairy and the Waif.*

The film was a success, and Miss Minter at her mother's insistence signed a contract to appear in six productions for Metro, *Always in the Way, Emmy of Stork's Nest, Barbara Frietchie, Dimples, Lovely Mary, Sally in Our Alley* (never released). Then in 1916, she was put under contract to American Flying A, for whom she made twenty-six films over the next three years. One of these, *The Ghost of Rosy Taylor,* is still in existence, and it is worth discussing at some length, as it is a typical programme picture of the decade, and also shows what a capable director the forgotten Edward Sloman must have been. (It is strange the way that the films of the decade's three greatest leading ladies have either vanished entirely or become so inaccessible.)

The Ghost of Rosy Taylor was five reels in length, scripted by Elizabeth Mahoney from a story by Josephine Daskam Bacon, and released in 1918. Mrs. Herriman-Smith (Marian Lee) meets her friend Mrs. Jeanne Du Vivier (Helen Howard) on the steps of the Metropolitan

Employment Agency. Mrs. Du Vivier thanks Mrs. Herriman-Smith for having recommended to her such an excellent charwoman as Rosy Taylor, but Mrs. Herriman-Smith is amazed because Rosy Taylor had since died. Mrs. Du Vivier insists that Rosy Taylor has cleaned the house for her every Saturday, although she has never seen the charwoman as she had always been away at the weekends. The two women decide to investigate, but when they reach the house they appear to see a ghost flapping at the window, hear the sound of clanking chains and hear Rosy Taylor's favourite song, "Old Black Joe," being sung. (The words of the song are superimposed on the picture, yet many historians claim that *Ben-Hur* in 1926 was the first time that superimposed titles were used.) The film then explains how this has all come about.

Rhoda Eldridge (Mary Miles Minter) and her father live in a cheap lodging house in a small French town. The father tells his daughter that they will never return to America, but will not give a reason. Rhoda goes out shopping in the market place, and there follow some delightful comedy scenes with a missing duck—Sloman has captured perfectly the atmosphere of a small suburban market place. While she is away, the father writes a letter, in which he tells Rhoda that her real name was Sayles, but that he had renounced the family name after a quarrel with his father and brother in America. The father dies, and it is learnt that Rhoda need never appeal to the family for assistance as the father had investments in the Transatlantic Marine Company, but a telegram arrives saying that the firm has been wiped out. Rhoda prepares to move to cheaper lodgings, but is suddenly, unexpectedly offered a position as a nursemaid to a family returning to America. However, when she reaches America she is told her services are no longer required.

Rhoda takes a room with Mrs. Sullivan (Kate Price) and for two weeks looks unsuccessfully for work. Then one day, sitting in the park, she finds a letter addressed to Rosy Taylor from Mrs. Du Vivier, appointing her as a charwoman and enclosing the key to the house. Rhoda discovers that Rosy Taylor is dead, goes to Mrs. Du Vivier's house, and begins to clean it.

Upstairs, Mrs. Du Vivier's brother, Jacques Le Clerc (Alan Forrest) is sleeping. When he awakes, he goes downstairs, and frightened Rhoda hides behind some curtains, where she is discovered. Jacques thinks that she is a burglar, and tells her that he will not report her to the police if she will promise to reform and go to a Protective Society, which he says will find her employment. Rhoda does as she is bid, but when the assistant at the Society reads the letter that Rhoda brings from Jacques, in which he said that he had caught her stealing, she pronounces Rhoda a menace to society, and has her sent to a reformatory. Sloman paints an impressive picture of a Protective Society in much the same way as Griffith shows the reformers in *Intolerance*. The Society tell two brothers that the elder is not capable of looking after the younger, who is sent to a Home, and a woman with a sick baby is turned away because it is not the right day for the Society to attend to babies.

At the reformatory, there is a disturbance, and Rhoda escapes. She returns to Mrs. Sullivan, who shields her from the Protective Society.

The next Saturday Rhoda goes back to the Du Vivier house, out of a need to earn money. However, the Protective Society tell Jacques of Rhoda's escape from the reformatory, and he goes home and finds Rhoda there. At this same moment, Mrs. Herriman-Smith and Mrs. Du Vivier meet—in the scene with which the film opened. Rhoda explains to Jacques what she was doing at the house, and shows him the letter from her father. Jacques goes to telephone the Protective Society, and after his departure Rhoda begins to clean the house at the same moment as the two women arrive. The ghost proves to be a duster on a pole to clean the windows, and the clanking chains are nothing more than a cat knocking over a bucket. Jacques is unable to get through to the Protective Society, and on his way back to the house meets the two terrified women.

Meanwhile, the police and a warden from the reformatory have arrived, and Rhoda is taken back to the Protective Society. Just as the head of the Protective Society is telling Rhoda that she must go back to the reformatory, Jacques and the women arrive, and it transpires that the head of the reformatory is the brother of Rhoda's father. Rhoda says that she does not wish to ask for his help, but he puts his arm round her and tells her that he wants to help her. Jacques prophesies that "The ghost of Rosy Taylor will haunt me for the rest of my life."

The picture has quite unbelievable charm, and Mary Miles Minter makes us forgive her lack of acting talent, by the sheer beauty of her face. Edward Sloman's direction is gentle and tender, as exemplified by the slow fades in and out as Rhoda tells in flashback her story to Jacques.

In 1919 Mary signed a contract with Adolph Zukor; her first production for Paramount was a tale ideally suited to her beauty, *Anne of Green Gables,* directed by William Desmond Taylor, with whom Miss Minter fell in love. Mary Miles Minter made twelve more films before February 1, 1922, the night on which William Desmond Taylor was murdered.

Much has been written about the murder of Taylor, many have speculated as to the murderer. This writer could not and does not wish to add anything further to what has been written. Obviously it was in many ways responsible for the end of the careers of Mabel Normand (who was the last person to see Taylor alive) and Mary Miles Minter (who was suspected of having an affair with Taylor). Without doubt, neither committed the murder, and neither were ever suspected of having committed the murder by the police. She made four more pictures for Paramount, and then her contract was terminated; Miss Minter was twenty-three years old. She is now a plump widow, Mrs. Brandon O'Hildebrandt, living in Los Angeles, more concerned with her income tax and real estate problems than with her film career.

The death of William Desmond Taylor in a way marked the end of an era; it was the end of Edward Wagenknecht's "age of innocence." A new era was opening in Hollywood; the era of the flapper, jazz and "it." Two years later, Ince would be dead; Griffith's career was declining. New men were taking over. Perhaps, as Kevin Brownlow claims, the Twenties were Hollywood's golden years, but there are many people who still believe that the cinema had reached its peak by 1919.

Bibliography

1   Marsh, Mae. *Screen Acting*. Los Angeles: Photo Star Publishing Co., 1921.

2   Barry, Iris and Eileen Bowser. *D. W. Griffith American Film Master*. New York: Museum of Modern Art, 1965.

3   Griffith, D. W. *The Rise and Fall of Free Speech in America*. Hollywood: Larry Edmunds Bookshop, 1967.

4   Dunham, Harold. *Mae Marsh and Robert Harron*. Unpublished manuscript.

5   Paine, Arthur Bigelow. *Life and Lillian Gish*. New York: Macmillan and Co., 1932.

6   Gaye, Howard. *So This Was Hollywood*. Unpublished manuscript in the possession of Mrs. Howard Gaye.

7   Agee, James. *Agee on Film*. New York: Beacon Press, 1958.

8   Wagenknecht, Edward. *The Movies in the Age of Innocence*. Norman: University of Oklahoma Press, 1962.

9   Loos, Anita. *A Girl Like I*. London: Hamish Hamilton, 1967. New York: Viking Press, 1966.

10 Robinson, Selma. "Don't Blame the Movies! Blame Life," *Motion Picture Magazine* (July 1926).

11 Griffith, D. W. "What I Demand of Movie Stars," *Motion Picture Magazine* (February 1917).

12 Brownlow, Kevin. *The Parade's Gone By*. London: Secker and Warburg, 1968. New York: Knopf, 1968.

13 Pickford, Mary. *Sunshine and Shadow*. London: Heinemann, 1956.

14 Arvidson, Linda. *When Movies Were Young*. New York: E. P. Dutton and Co., 1925.

15 Stern, Seymour. *Index to the Creative Work of D. W. Griffith*. London: The British Film Institute, 1944–47.

16 ———. "The Cold War Against D. W. Griffith," *Films in Review* (February 1956).

17 ———. "Biographical Hogwash," *ibid* (May and June/July 1959).

18 ———. "The Birth of a Nation," *Film Culture* (Spring-Summer 1965).

19   Gish, Lillian. *The Movies, Mr. Griffith and Me.* London: W. H. Allen and Co., 1969. New York: Prentice-Hall, 1969.

20   Henderson, R. M. *The Role of D .W. Griffith in the Development of the Dramatic Motion Picture 1908–1913.* Unpublished thesis for a Doctorate in Philosophy.

21   O'Dell, Paul. "The Birth of a Nation," *The Silent Picture* (Autumn 1969).

22   Sweet, Blanche. "Judith of Bethulia," *The Silent Picture* (Winter 1969/70).

23   Ellis, Frederick J. "The Passing of a Great Showman," *Story World* (January 1925).

24   Ince, Thomas H. "The Art of Motion Picture Directing," *Pictures and the Picturegoer* (August 10, 1918).

25   ———. "The Early Days of Kay Bee," *Photoplay* (March 1919).

26   ———. "Memoirs of Thomas H. Ince," *Exhibitors' Herald* (December 13, 1924–January 10, 1925).

27   Mitchell, George. "Thomas H. Ince," *Films in Review* (October 1960).

28   Mitry, Jean. *Ince.* Paris: Anthologie du Cinéma, 1965.

29   Pratt, George C. "See Mr. Ince," *Image* (May 1956).

30   ———. *Spellbound in Darkness.* Rochester: University School of Liberal and Applied Studies, 1966.

34   Bodeen, DeWitt. "Marguerite Clark," *Films in Review* December 1964.

35   ———. "Charles Ray," *ibid* (November 1968).

36   Ussher, Kathleen. "Re-enter Charles Ray," *Picturegoer* (October 1926).

37   Ramsaye, Terry. *A Million and One Nights.* New York: Simon and Schuster Inc., 1926. Reprinted (1964) by Frank Cass and Co. Ltd. (London).

38   Card, James. "The Films of Mary Pickford," *Image* (December 1959).

39   Hall, Alice. "Marguerite Make-Believe," *Picturegoer* (April 1921).

40   Ames, Aydelott. "Mary Miles Minter," *Films in Review* (October 1969).

41   Irwin, W. *The House that Shadows Built*. New York: Doubleday, Doran and Company Inc., 1928.

42   Goldwyn, Samuel. *Behind the Screen*. New York: George H. Doran Company, 1923.

Index

(to films of the period and personalities; major film references in bold type)

162

163